THE EVERGLADES

*Stories of Grit and Spirit
from the Mangrove Wilderness*

ANNE McCRARY SULLIVAN
AND HOLLY GENZEN

Pineapple
Press

PALM BEACH, FLORIDA

**Pineapple
Press**

An imprint of Globe Pequot, the trade division of
The Rowman & Littlefield Publishing Group, Inc.
4501 Forbes Blvd., Ste. 200
Lanham, MD 20706
PineapplePress.com

Distributed by NATIONAL BOOK NETWORK

British Library Cataloguing in Publication Information Available

Library of Congress Cataloging-in-Publication Data

978-1-68334-092-8 (cloth)
978-1-68334-095-9 (electronic)

∞™ The paper used in this publication meets the minimum requirements of
American National Standard for Information Sciences—Permanence of Paper for
Printed Library Materials, ANSI/NISO Z39.48-1992.

For my sons, Kenyata and Jolyon,

who may never go out there but who love

that their mother does.

— A n n e

_____

For Gary, David, and Jonathan,

with love.

— H o l l y

Mangrove prop roots. Photograph by Anne McCrary Sullivan.

CONTENTS

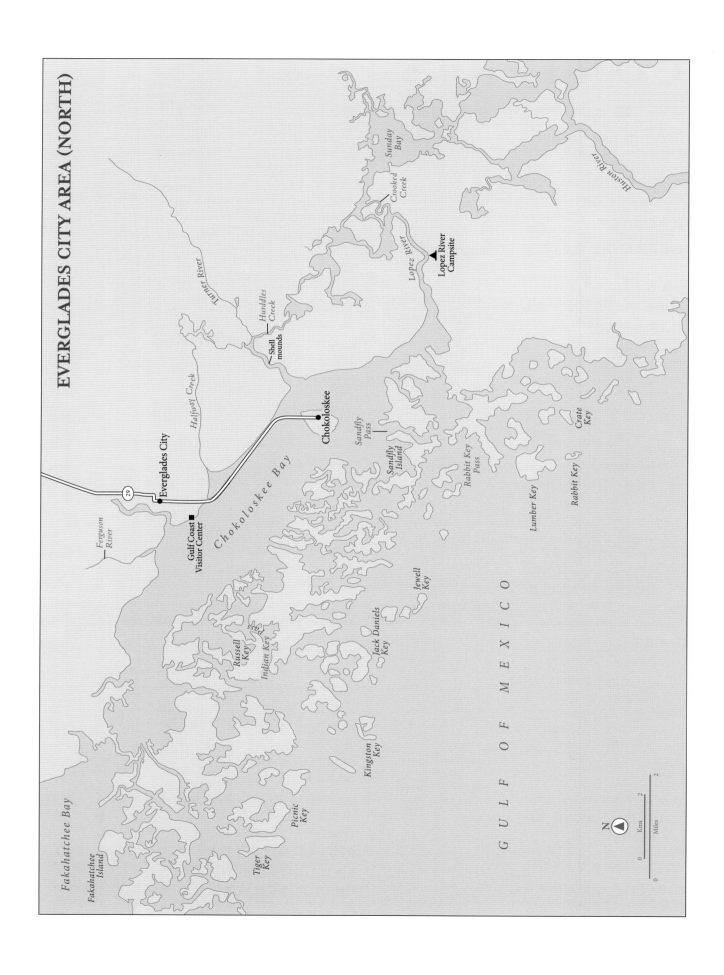

EVERGLADES CITY AREA (NORTH)

Fakahatchee Bay

Fakahatchee Island

Ferguson River

Halfway Creek

Turner River

Huddles Creek

Shell mounds

Everglades City

29

Gulf Coast Visitor Center

Chokoloskee

Chokoloskee Bay

Sandfly Pass

Sandfly Island

Lopez River

Lopez River Campsite

Crooked Creek

Sunday Bay

Huston River

Rabbit Key Pass

Russell Key

Indian Key Pass

Jack Daniels Key

Jewell Key

Kingston Key

Picnic Key

Tiger Key

Lumber Key

Rabbit Key

Crate Key

GULF OF MEXICO

N

Kms   2

0

Miles   2

0

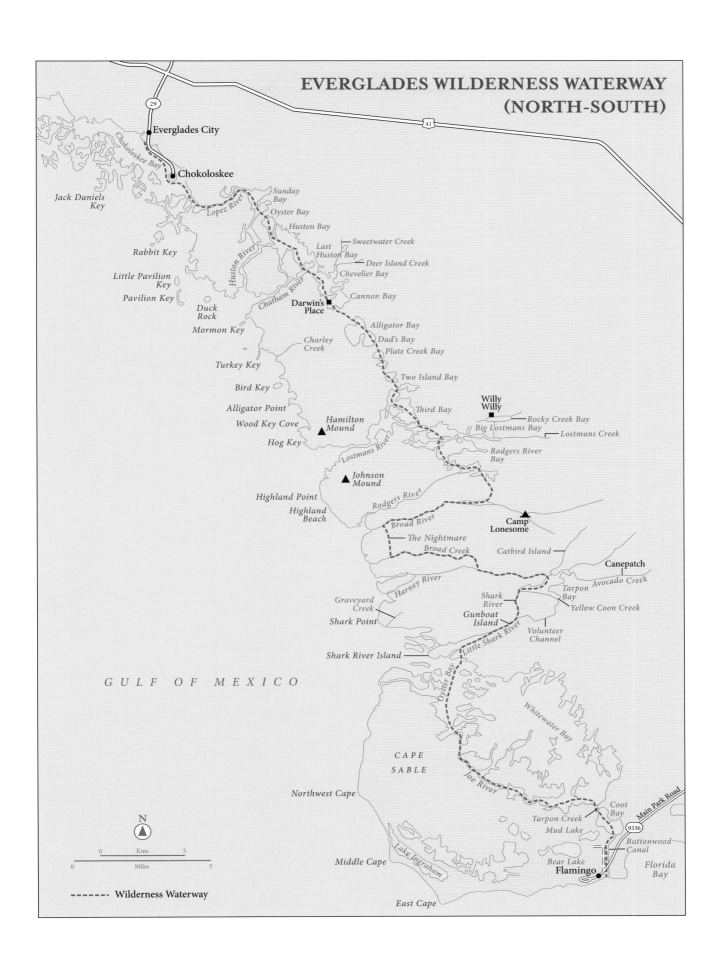

EVERGLADES WILDERNESS WATERWAY (NORTH-SOUTH)

29

41

Everglades City

Chokoloskee

Chokoloskee Bay

Jack Daniels Key

Lopez River

Sunday Bay

Oyster Bay

Huston Bay

Rabbit Key

Little Pavilion Key

Pavilion Key

Duck Rock

Mormon Key

Huston River

Chatham River

Sweetwater Creek

Last Huston Bay

Deer Island Creek

Chevelier Bay

Cannon Bay

Darwin's Place

Alligator Bay

Dad's Bay

Plate Creek Bay

Charley Creek

Turkey Key

Bird Key

Two Island Bay

Alligator Point

Wood Key Cove

▲ Hamilton Mound

Third Bay

Willy Willy ■

Rocky Creek Bay

Big Lostmans Bay

Lostmans Creek

Hog Key

Lostmans River

Rodgers River Bay

▲ Johnson Mound

Highland Point

Highland Beach

Rodgers River

Broad River

▲ Camp Lonesome

The Nightmare

Broad Creek

Catbird Island

Canepatch

Avocado Creek

Harney River

Shark River

Tarpon Bay

Yellow Coon Creek

Graveyard Creek

Shark Point

Gunboat Island

Volunteer Channel

Shark River Island

Little Shark River

GULF OF MEXICO

Oyster Bay

Whitewater Bay

CAPE SABLE

Northwest Cape

Joe River

Coot Bay

Main Park Road

Tarpon Creek

9336

Mud Lake

Buttonwood Canal

Lake Ingraham

Middle Cape

Bear Lake

Flamingo

Florida Bay

East Cape

N
▲

0 — Kms — 5

0 — Miles — 5

- - - - - Wilderness Waterway

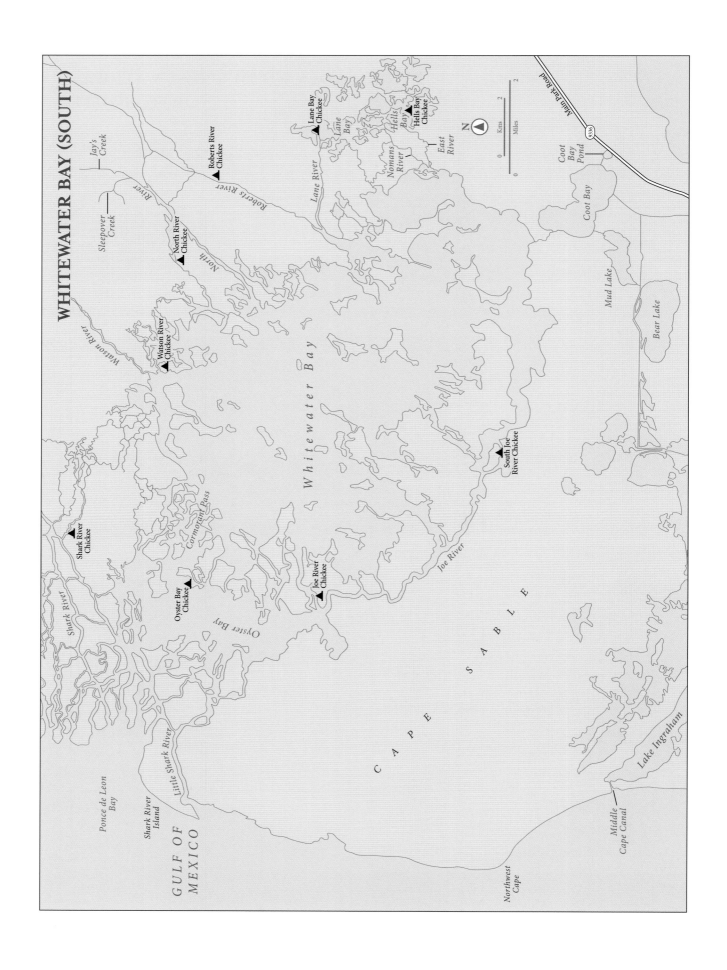

WHITEWATER BAY (SOUTH)

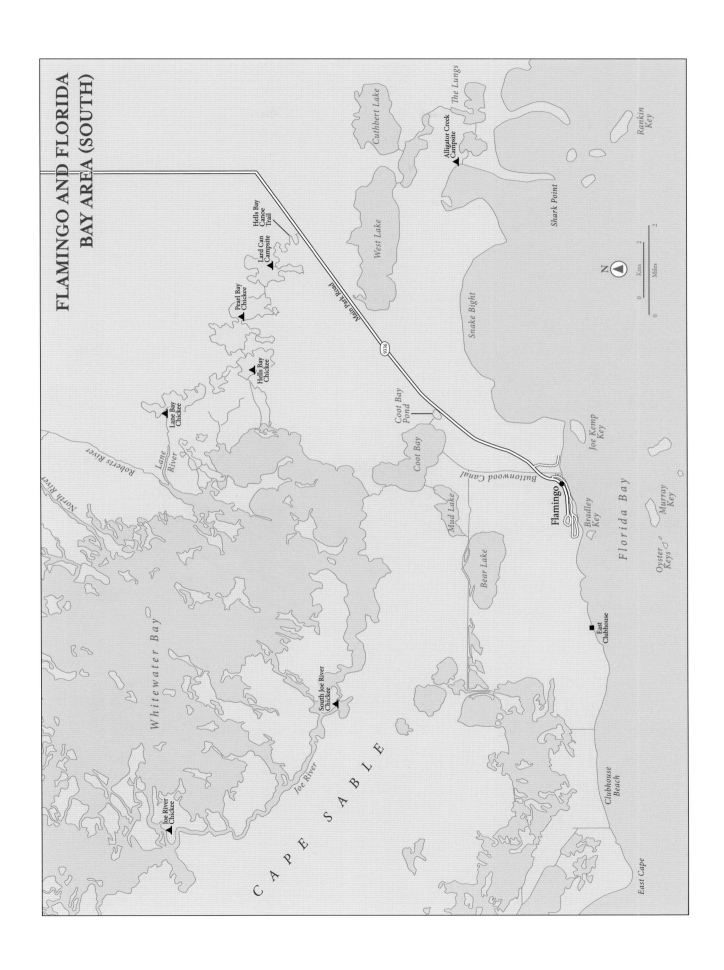

FLAMINGO AND FLORIDA BAY AREA (SOUTH)

PREFACE

During the years when we were paddling the mangrove wilderness of Everglades National Park and writing *Paddling the Everglades Wilderness Waterway* (Genzen and Sullivan 2011), we met some adventurous people who told fascinating stories. One evening, soon after the book had been accepted for publication, we sat on overturned buckets at Alligator Point listening to Bill Leonard, in his seventies, talking about coming down from Maine year after year to paddle the Waterway. When we went back inside our tent, we looked at each other, each with the same thought: we've got another book to write. A few months later, Holly interviewed Bill at his home in Maine. In California, Anne interviewed William G. Truesdell whose guidebook to the Everglades Wilderness Waterway had been our constant companion while we were writing a guidebook of our own. The process of writing this book was underway.

For a period of several years, each pursuing other projects, we continued interviewing people who had significant experience of the mangrove wilderness that fringes the interface of land and salt water in Everglades National Park. At first, the idea was to talk with paddlers, but it expanded to include wildlife managers, naturalists, park rangers, park volunteers, an archaeologist, and others. When geography and timing allowed, we conducted interviews jointly; otherwise, we conducted them separately. Interviews were conversational and varied considerably in length, from one hour to sixteen hours (in multiple sessions).

In addition to our lives as naturalists and paddlers, we are both social scientists retired from academic lives, each bringing research propensities into this project. We were committed to allowing our participants to speak for themselves and retain ownership of their stories. We did our own transcription, made all selections, and shaped them into a narrative in each participant's voice. Each participant received both the transcript and the highly edited story we shaped from their own words. We invited them to delete what they wanted, add anything they wanted, make corrections, and otherwise collaborate in shaping their story. Some were very involved; others left it primarily up to us. The result is a collection of twenty-one crafted oral histories, each revealing a different voice telling a unique story.

The unedited transcripts are rich in park and personal history, not all of which would fit into the pages of this book. The transcripts will be placed in the archives at Everglades National Park where they will be available to future researchers.

It has been a privilege to do this work and an honor to listen to these voices. We are grateful to all who accepted the invitation to tell us how and why their lives have led them into the Everglades mangrove wilderness.

Mangrove with stormy sky. Photograph by Anne McCrary Sullivan.

Beach spider-lily, Picnic Key. Photograph by Holly Genzen.

INTRODUCTION

OUT THERE

A wilderness, in contrast with those areas where man and his own works dominate the landscape, is hereby recognized as an area where the earth and its community of life are untrammeled by man, where man himself is a visitor who does not remain.

—The Wilderness Act of 1964

Everglades National Park's mangrove wilderness, extending more than 230,000 acres, is the most expansive in the Western Hemisphere and the largest continuous system of mangroves in the world. This mangrove-scape is dynamic, constantly changing with the forces of tide and wind, shifting depositions of sand and mud, the slow, continuous fall of senescent leaves, the rich accumulation of detritus that transforms repeatedly through food webs, becomes the source of life in its branches, its roots, its waters, and the air above the mangal—fin, wing, carapace, jelly. Islands are born and islands disappear—or simply change their size and shape. Hurricanes sometimes divide an island, splitting it in two. Nothing is static out there.

Most of these overwashed mangrove islands have no land at all, only sulphurous muds exposed at low tide, then covered by salty tides again. And again. And again. Muds are stitched together by an interlacing network of prop roots.

Most of what can be called land out there, beyond the mainland's mangrove fringe, was created by early peoples of the Glades, people who constructed shell mounds—not simply middens, not accumulations of randomly cast-off materials, but systematically engineered communities of mounds, which archaeologists like Margo Schwadron are now discovering to be far more complex than has previously been understood. These, too, are ringed by mangroves.

There are no roads. To get out there one must take a fish route or a bird route: go by boat—kayak, canoe, or motorboat—or fly in via plane or helicopter. Apart from designated campsites on a few scattered shell mounds, if you want to pitch a tent, you'll need to follow riverine mangroves or chains of mangrove islands to the Gulf beaches. Or, to remain on the interior, reserve a chickee, a wooden

Buttonwood with bromeliad. Photograph by Holly Genzen.

platform constructed over water with open sides and a slanted roof, provided by Everglades National Park.

The voices in this book tell stories of going out there. Some speak from early days in Everglades National Park. Bill Truesdell remembers mapping and marking the Everglades Wilderness Waterway, then writing the first guidebook for that ninety-nine-mile water trail. Ralph Miele, first ranger pilot in the National Park Service, tells stories of flying with politicians and scientists over remote mangrove wilderness areas when the park was still being shaped and biological studies just beginning. Wanda Brown Townsend remembers a time before there was a national park when her aunts, uncles, cousins, and grandparents lived on Fakahatchee Island just beyond what is now the park boundary. Oron "Sonny" Bass and Leon Howell also remember growing up at a mangrove fringe before there was a national park, then ultimately coming to work at the park.

No one goes out there without specifically wanting to. This is a book about people who want to. Some go for work, some for adventure, some for philosophy, some for science. But the people represented in this book defy easy categorization. Tony Terry, the law enforcement ranger who patrols the mangroves as part of his job, goes back out on his days off to release the tensions of the job, to fish, to find peace—"It's my shrink." Lichen researchers, Rick and Jean Seavey, go out for fieldwork, yet they speak of the context in which they work as "spiritual." Supervisory park ranger, Susan Reece, loves to put her hands in the mangrove muck. Roger Hammer, the expert in plants of the Everglades, goes out there not so much to look at plants, all of which he calls intimately by their scientific and common names, but because he loves to catch and cook a fat redfish, have a fine meal with a glass of Merlot in deep wilderness—because he loves solitude.

Many of these voices speak of solitude. Ann Rougle, solo paddler, speaks of "glorious solitude" and being "blissfully stranded." Tom Buttle echoes, "Getting stranded here isn't a bad thing." Rick Horton, calling those strings of islands "a kayaker's rosary," says that for him, "time spent alone in the wilderness is a time of spiritual redemption."

Some speak of companionship. Sometimes it's the companionship of a life partner, sometimes a fishing buddy or a group of friends. Bill Leonard talks about heading out with groups of twelve or more to paddle the Everglades Wilderness Waterway. Eco-adventure guide, John Lewis, attends to the varying interests and experience levels of small groups who explore the mangroves close to Chokoloskee Island. Many miles deeper in the mangroves, John and Donna Buckley greet paddlers and entertain guests on their houseboat, the *Swamp Lily*.

Some go to fish. Some never fish. JohnBob Carlos used to go for the fish, but little by little began leaving the fishing rod at home, taking the camera. Leon Howell fishes but he has "long since quit caring whether I caught fish or not."

Many speak of being tested, of meeting challenges of tide, wind, weather, equipment failure, getting lost, sheltering from storms, or recovery from one's own errors.

Most say that no matter how many times you go, no matter how long you stay, there is always an element of surprise, something unexpected. "Every time there is something new," says photographer Constance Mier.

The one thing these storytellers have in common is that they didn't just go once. Their stories are replete with accounts of stranding, being lost, being besieged by insects, struggling in the elements, suffering discomforts. But as Toby Nipper reminds us, "Attitude is the difference between an adventure or an ordeal." In spite of, or maybe even because of, the challenges, these voices speak passionately about being "out there," and going back.

We keep going back too. And we have sometimes asked ourselves why. We've been out there for days, muscles aching, a cold front moving in, no-see-ums appearing in swarms; storms moving across South Florida and lightning flashing all around us; or sleeping in the canoe because wind has blown the water out of our shallow bay. And we ask, "Now, why is it we keep wanting to come back out here?"

The answer to that question may be floating in our genetic ancestry, some remnant of profound connection with the wild that lingers and, in spite of challenges and discomforts, makes wilderness feel, as Vivian Oliva says, like home. There is something profound about being out there. And no matter what discomforts we may experience in any given trip, no matter how glad we may be to have that first shower when we get back, within weeks we are talking about when we might head out there again. Because "out there," we are somehow stabilized, somehow reconnected with the very origins of life on earth, its rhythms and cycles of life and death, moving tides and changing skies. A dolphin swims up to the chickee where we are sitting at the end of the day, stops, lifts its head out of water, looks at us, and we know that somehow, we are connected. Everything, all of us, are connected.

For a number of years, wildlife biologist Skip Snow's assignment in Everglades National Park was to learn as much as possible about the exotic pythons that have taken up residence there. He says, "I have thought about writing a book in which you would learn stuff about pythons in the park, but it wouldn't be like a chapter on how they reproduce and then a chapter on what they eat. . . . It would be a book about places, kind of like Dr. Seuss in that book, *All the Places You'll Go*, right? The places that pythons led me, the different roads I went down, like a travelogue through the

Lone paddler, Pearl Bay. Photograph by Holly Genzen.

python encounters. But you would come out of my book knowing something about pythons." We feel we have written a similar book about mangroves. There are no specific chapters on how they grow, how they reproduce, or the ecological role they play. Rather there are stories of mangrove places, voices of people who go there for a wide variety of reasons. We believe that through these voices, through stories of adventure, investigation, and inspiration, we learn something about our Everglades mangrove wilderness.

We know that there are many more stories than our little net could catch. We think of this book as good reading for now but also as a resource for future researchers. As a storied account of human interactions with the mangrove wilderness, it offers material for the social history of a remote place, a place so inhospitable and inaccessible that few venture there, but those who do tend to go again and again, seeking something they sometimes struggle to name, something still wild, still free.

Evening, Lane Bay. Photograph by Anne McCrary Sullivan.

The Buckleys' houseboat, Swamp Lily II, *in one of their frequent moorings near the North River. Photograph by Anne McCrary Sullivan.*

PART I

LOOK WHERE I GET TO WORK!

SEASONS ON THE *SWAMP LILLY*
The Buckleys

BACKCOUNTRY VOLUNTEERS, EVERGLADES NATIONAL PARK

The first time we laid eyes on the Everglades, we were guides. Had a paying group of people we brought down here, and we had never laid eyes on the place. But we pulled it off. I mean, we knew what to do. We saw what tour companies were offering, and we just did that. For ten years we did that. And then we felt we didn't need that extra revenue during the winter. We wanted to come down ourselves. We'd always been looking back in these nooks and crannies in the mangroves as we went by them. We thought if we had a little houseboat, we could put it back in there and just really have a good time.

We decided, okay, we're going to get us a pontoon boat. And we're going to build a little house on it. We'll take it down there, and we'll offer to stay out there and help to look after the place.

Donna: We'd be the eyes and ears.

John: Stewardship was the word that we used. We invented the role.

We didn't even know that there was a volunteer program. So we wrote, said we're going to come, we're going to stay for the winter, help you with the stewardship of the place. We're pretty competent at this. We can work remote and unsupervised.

This guy being the way he was, he didn't answer our letter. So we've built this little house on a pontoon boat, and we're pulling it down the road into the park, coming down the Main Park Road. This guy drives up in his Park Service pickup, and we see his jaw is dropping. He should have answered that letter. So he says, "You can't do this. You can't come down and live here."

Donna: So I pulled out a copy of the letter that we wrote.

John: I told him, "Well, we rented out our house, had our dog put to sleep, and we're going to have to work this out somehow." Not that we really had the dog put to sleep. In fact, we didn't even rent our house. But he said, okay, just go out in the backcountry, as far out as you can get, and keep your head down. In a few weeks, come back in, and we'll see if we've got this worked out.

Oh, it was a great three weeks out here! We had the best time of our lives. We fished and paddled and swam and listened to the gators bellow. It was just fantastic.

East Cape Sable. Photograph by Holly Genzen.

In three weeks we went back. The guy had some paperwork. "Sign here, and you are volunteers in the park. Just go out there and just do what you're doing and go to campsites and make sure people aren't playing fast and loose with the permits." We said, well, it sounds like fun. That was twenty-nine years ago.

Our knowledge and our duties for the park have evolved over the years. Now we're intertwined with practically every division in the park. We're under the umbrella of law enforcement, but we've also worked with research. For instance, they would have us check water salinity, give us instruments, and we would keep records. We helped Florida Fisheries, monitoring alligators, crocodiles, bats. We kept track of osprey nests and eagle nests.

Donna: Eventually we were working with Skip Snow, keeping track of manatees. Skip gave me a map of their backs. So whenever we'd see a manatee, we had these forms to fill out. What was the sky like? What were the weather conditions? Were there any markings on the manatee itself?

John: Search and rescue has become a big thing for us. *Anybody* can get lost out here! I've been lost more than once. You're going along in the motorboat and see someone you want to make contact with, and then maybe you're giving them some gas or something, and you've got your head down, looking in their boat, waves spinning your boat, bouncing you around, and when it's over, you look up and. . . . Where am I? Which way is east, west, north, south?

I see people, they've got a map, they're looking at an island here, an island here, finding their route, saying, "That makes sense." But they get out on the water, and what they're looking at is *this* (holds the map at eye level, looks horizontally). And there are a lot of little islands on the chart that are no longer there. Water comes in, goes out, lapping at edges, undermines a tree, the tree falls in. Water gets more access to the bank. Next thing you know, another tree falls in. A lot of islands are gone. Just gone. Over the years, every time we go by Gunboat Island, it's smaller. It's going to disappear someday.

But, say someone is lost. If we know they were going from this campsite to that campsite, we know the route well enough to know where probably they went wrong. We can go back in there at night, shine a big light up in the air, make noise, blow whistles, and usually get them out, prevent the park from having to go into an expensive search.

We've begun a new thing this year. When we see paddlers on the water who look like they're on a trip, we go right to them, introduce ourselves, make sure everything is going well. We find that people like to show us their permits 'cause they're proud of them, and they like to talk about their kayak or canoe and tell us their other

adventures. They know right away that we are advocates for paddlers. By doing that, we have had hardly any call outs. We talk to people and prevent it.

Often our work is just managing little things. Like a few weeks ago a couple of guys thought they were checking in, using their SPOT, but it wasn't working right. So their dad was concerned and called. We went and found them.

The next morning, we went by Lane Bay Chickee, turned left, started down the Lane River. Three guys in a powerboat had got into this big shallow bay and got stuck. Their engine sucked in a bunch of mud, was overheating. We fixed their motor, got the mud out.

Then we were going up to Tarpon Bay through an area we call Shot in the Dark 'cause it's where you jump from the big Coast Guard markers in Cormorant Pass to the little waterway markers. You have to stay right on track 'cause over on the right is a big mud flat and sure enough, a fishing boat was high and dry on that. He wasn't standing up and frantically waving, he was just waiting for the tide to come in. So we called dispatch to say if there's an overdue boater, we know where he is.

Then over at Canepatch, two guys and their two little boys came in, and they said, "Oh, we didn't know you needed a reservation," which is a lie because they've been here before. I said, "We're not going to make you leave, but we'll get your name and your phone number and the numbers off your boat, and on your way out of the park, stop and pay for the use of this place. If you don't, you get a ticket." So they got to stay, they didn't look like fools in the eyes of their little boys, and the park gets the twenty bucks or so.

So there are a lot of little things like that. Then there are things that don't happen often, thankfully. One night, one stormy, rainy night we were on the *Swamp Lily*, like we are now, anchored up in the Hells Bay area. It was gray and overcast and nasty, foggy, and misty, and all of a sudden there was this one thunder that didn't sound like the rest of them. "What was *that*?" Then, on the park radio, a dispatch said a plane had gone off the radar really close to our location. So we went roaring up this river with a boat with a light. Donna yelled out, "There's wreckage in the water."

Donna: We could smell the jet fuel.

John: And we ended up being the first ones on scene. A double fatality.

Donna: You know, when you start out, you're hoping you're going to be plucking someone out of the water and saving them.

John: For days after that, we were picking up the people in little pieces, literally. Little pieces of people. A pretty hard thing to do. But that's only happened once. So if you want to know what the typical winter is like out here, there isn't one. And there's always something major and bizarre that happens, and you just don't know what it's going to be this year.

Donna: It's been kind of quiet lately.

John: But we look for stuff! We look for stuff! You ever know a hunting dog that didn't want to hunt?

Donna: There's always little stuff.

The people got the keys to this park in 1947, right? And at that time, it was a huge park. To come where we are now was an expedition, not to be taken lightly. The boats then went ten to fifteen miles per hour tops, if you had a nice boat. This was a big, big park. To get into the heartland of it, people had to make plans and take time to get here, and when they did a successful trip, they were proud of themselves. They learned something. They had found their way and had a great experience camping, fishing. And they were different people when they got back. They had been changed by it.

But the boats got faster and faster. Now, they're going sixty, seventy, eighty miles an hour, coming from both ends of the park, and the park is small. You zip to the middle of the park, zip back, and you don't hear anything, can hardly see anything while you're doing that. People come from Fort Lauderdale to Tarpon Bay and catch a fish and they're back home to watch the evening news. They think it's how this park was meant to be used. Meanwhile, we have paddlers still trying to use it in a traditional, self-propelled, low-impact manner.

The park says it was traditional to have powerboats and we need to allow traditional use. But eighty miles an hour, one hour to get from Flamingo to Everglades City is not "traditional." The people who are paddling it; they are doing a traditional use.

Everglades National Park is *the best* place there is to paddle in the wintertime. Anywhere we go or anchor, we paddle. But there are paddlers who sanitize their trip, so they are totally cocooned in safety. Before they left, they Google-Earthed where they were going and saw everything that they were going to see. They have a satellite phone and a SPOT and GPS. Don't they want to discover anything? So maybe I am an opinionated old fart! But it gets to the point where, why go? Just read about it, see it on your screen.

And there's nothing out here that's going to hurt you. There's nothing to fall off of. There's nothing that's going to eat you. Unless you're already dead. You're not going to freeze to death. And it's not *that* hot. I mean if it gets to ninety degrees, you're on top of water, which is much cooler. Sprinkle water on your head and you cool right off. And if you get lost, me and Donna will come get you.

John: I was telling some park people as we were paddling down the Jungle Trail that there was a person that they let get away without telling his story. His name was Ed Stefanic. He was one of the original nine employees of the park. He's the one that laid out the Hells Bay Canoe Trail. That must have been a mind-boggling task. He continued to come down here every winter, I think, into his eighties. We would find his little commando campsites out in the backcountry where he would find himself a paurotis palm island or something to make a camp on. He had a little aluminum boat with an outboard motor, and he would go back there all by himself and fish. We always hoped to run into him. He was elusive 'cause he was out of regulation out there. All we wanted to do was talk to him. When they opened the park, he was a ranger running around trying to catch poachers.

When we first began bringing groups down here for a five- or six-day trip, we might see *an* alligator. It made the trip. The last of the alligators were hiding deep in the backcountry. Those original rangers would go out and chase the poachers, make life difficult for them. But what saved alligators was making it illegal to buy or to sell hides. When laws took away the ability for poachers to market what they poached, there was no longer a reason to do it. Conservation works. Now, the remaining nucleus of alligators has swelled out, and there's a reason why when you leave this park, at your retirement, they give you a wooden alligator. It's the landmark symbol of the Everglades, and that's because we saved the last of them.

There was this guy that went around to all of the states and determined the most remote spot in the state, furthest away from any manmade structure. The most remote spot in Florida is Highland Beach. That's where the whales beached themselves.

We overheard a call on the radio. A guy had spotted four whales on the beach. So we jump in this powerboat and head down there. Coming into Highland Beach, we could see big black objects up on the sand. We stopped maybe one hundred yards off the beach. I hopped out and got into the Monarch, my canoe-kayak thing.

Donna: My role was to stay on the park radio, stay in contact with dispatch. I had just had hip replacement surgery, so I wasn't about to jump in and try to wrestle whales.

John: She was monitoring the whales that were still offshore, a compact group of maybe thirty or forty whales.

Donna: They weren't moving. They were just kind of hanging out.

John: Up on the beach I found more than four whales, most of them partway in the water. I picked out the liveliest looking one, got in the water and got ahold of him by the tail. It felt fantastic! Like a high-quality rubber mat, wet, but firm to grab to. There's enough cartilage, I guess, in the tail, and no slime like on a fish. When whales flap, they flap up and down, rather than side to side like a fish, so my arms were going up and down, and I was wiggling him this way, wiggling him that way, rocking him and pulling him in the water, and everything was working out well. But when you have them on their side, they're no longer going up and down. Next time he wanted to flap—boom! he just launched my ass right out into the water. That was exciting.

Donna: And I'm standing there going, "Oh, John!"

John: Once I realized that was the way it was, it didn't happen anymore. I got a couple of them in the water, and then some help from Everglades City showed up. We got some whales off the shore, but some would make a little loop and head back in. We'd go out and meet them, redirect them, and start them off again. But they didn't have any great enthusiasm for getting back into the Gulf. And the pod didn't have any enthusiasm for leaving.

After we got five off and left four that were obviously dead or would be dead soon, we had to get back home. But Donna had gotten information out over the radio about the pod there and the beached whales. The next day we got a call saying there would be NOAA veterinarians coming and we were to meet them halfway. I'd say we met eleven boats there—park rangers, Fish and Wildlife folks, NOAA, and the Coast Guard.

Donna: And pretty soon there were helicopters, TV channels. It was a zoo!

John: That day, we got in boats behind the pod and spent hours gently herding them out to sea. I paddled right on the edge of the pod with the whale I figured was the leader. We were eye to eye for hours.

Donna: They made little squeaking noises.

John: Yeah. Communicated with each other. By the end of the day, we got most of the pod into water deep enough that they were not going to run aground.

Donna: They were pilot whales. Beautiful. All black.

John: The one that I was right alongside forever, he could have knocked me over if he wanted to. But he was very gentle. We were just in it, you know, together.

When we first came here, we came to paddle. Then we really got into fishing and exploring, getting back where nobody else can fish. We were kind of secretive about the really good spots that we found, but we've learned now that the most fun we can have with our knowledge is to tell other people where to find some fish. Last year there was a boatload of guys up on Tarpon Bay and we watched them fishing in the wrong places. Finally, after hours of not catching tarpon on Tarpon Bay, they motored over to our boat and asked us, "What's up with this?"

We explained, well, you're fishing like everyone else does. You're fishing the shoreline, thinking all the fish are hiding in the mangrove roots. There are a bunch of big tarpon out there, but they are behind you, about 150 yards off shore. Go fish out there and see what happens. They weren't gone for five minutes before they were whooping and hollering, six-foot-long fish jumping up in the air.

And the most fun you can get with a nice cold beer is to bring on board a hot and tired paddler, give 'em a cold beer. And just watch 'em, you know. A lot of times they'll just hold it on their head for a while.

The Everglades in the winter is home for us now. We've been coming here for so many years. We move the houseboat around in the Flamingo district, have anchorage spots in different areas. Each spot is special. And it's home.

Usually, we're in Otter Creek. It was the first place we came when we began to do this. This is a nice deep river with relatively fresh water, a good mix of wildlife and variety of trees. But we have some other spots we like to be. There's an island down the bay that we call Catbird Island because it is just full of catbirds. So many of these islands are not named, and you spend a lot of time saying, "You know that little island next to the place where the creek comes out and there's a green tree there?" So we named this Catbird Island.

And there's Yellow Coon Creek. One year, a long time ago, there was a commotion going on up in a tree. We were paddling by, looking, and this really old raccoon, his coat just blonde, had his head buried in a bromeliad. It had finally rained after a dry spell, and he was trying to get something to drink. He evidently was deaf and blind because we were making all this noise, and he didn't even know we were there. We watched him for a long time, and that's how we came to name Yellow Coon Creek. Sometimes we'll get a call from the rangers and they'll ask where we are. "We're at Yellow Coon Creek." They don't have the nerve to say they don't know where that is.

We've named Catbird Creek, Yellow Coon Creek, Volunteer Channel, the Jungle Trail, and Sleepover Creek. A friend of ours got himself lost while he was out fishing, had to spend the night in his boat. So that's how Sleepover Creek got named.

John: Holy shit, look at that!

Donna: Moon's coming up. It's a golden color. That's beautiful.

John: And look over your right shoulder at the dark band between the mangroves and the water. We had a nice high tide, and it's beginning to drop. This is a

land where you get rivers that run one way for six hours and another way for the next six hours.

We experience a lot of things out here. But we also miss a lot. I almost missed that moon. You have to be here a long time to witness the things that can happen here because you'll be looking the other way when something goes by, or there'll be a big splash right beside the boat, and someone will say *What was that?!* A lot goes unnoticed. But if you're here long enough, you get lucky like this.

One night we were sitting here on the *Swamp Lily*, out in the mangroves on a night like this, and there was a knock on the door. Two guys from Michigan were trying to find North River Chickee, and they had seen our light. They paddled right up here and knocked on the door.

Donna: Gives you a bit of a start, a knock on the door, way out here.

You know, we've gotten lost out here. We've found our way out. We've caught fish, not caught fish. We've camped in good weather, bad weather. We've been really hot and really cold. Big winds. Wishing the wind would blow.

There's a spot on the North River we call our hurricane hole. We've never been here during hurricane season, but we've experienced some big storms, hurricane strength winds. We take the houseboat between some islands and tie up several different ways. More than once we've been in there and we could feel the boat lift up from the water and come back down, lift up and come back down. And we've looked out the door in a black, black storm, seen whitecaps coming up the North River. It feels really good to be in the hurricane hole when that happens.

In the park's booklet about the volunteer program, there's a Volunteer's Bill of Rights. One of them says you've got the right to be exposed to new experiences and to learn things. We've had a number of good managers that have exposed us to new experiences and made us a stronger tool for the park, and it's kept our interest up. That's why we're here after twenty-nine winters.

Black mangrove at Florida Bay. Photograph by Anne McCrary Sullivan.

IT'S ALL ABOUT PROTECTION

Tony Terry

LAW ENFORCEMENT RANGER, EVERGLADES NATIONAL PARK

When I went to college, I wanted to go into a profession that would help Black folks out. Black people. At that time, we needed more lawyers to help people get out of trouble, so my major was criminal justice. And then I changed to wanting to be an FBI agent, get more minorities in the FBI. And all that went to hell when I came down to the Glades and fell in love with the water and South Beach and all those things. I was a young guy when I came here, twenty-two.

My job here is law enforcement and resource protection. When I first came here in May 1992, as a backcountry ranger, my boss told me if I could get John Buckley to mentor me, I would learn a lot. I met with John and Donna and worked with them as a team. We rode all over this place, paddling or in powerboats, and they got me lost a lot. John would take me out in twisty areas of Hells Bay, Watson River, and say, "Okay, now get us back."

You know, as a ranger, one of the things you learn is that you never really know your way around the backcountry. And if you get too cocky, you're gonna mess up a boat, you're gonna get lost, embarrass yourself. So I'm still learning.

Learning the basic job of rescuing people, that took time. Maybe five years to get to where when someone explains they're lost, and they're explaining silly stuff, like "I just made a sharp turn in a river, and the last place I remember is the Lane River Chickee." Well, how long ago was that? Five hours. So they're nowhere near the Lane River Chickee. I mean, it took about five years to learn to listen to people and figure out where they are, so I can put up an airplane or a helicopter or go out there.

A lot of folks get lost coming down from Lane Bay into Hells Bay. With me, I'm using a compass mostly. The compass is real basic. You know, I get a general heading coming in, and I make sure I'm on the opposite heading coming back out. Chart and compass are reliable. GPS is good, but sometimes you can't take enough batteries, or they just do weird stuff. But once you've challenged yourself with chart and compass, and you know you can do that, GPS can make you relax more.

We have complete jurisdiction here. It's called concurrent jurisdiction. We work with the agencies around us, and we work with pretty much everything Miami-Dade deals with. Human smuggling was a regular thing for a while. The go-fast boats have been known to come in here, drop people at Cape Sable, but mostly they dropped them at Dry Tortugas. Smugglers would get $10,000 per head, more or less. We busted some pretty mean people, and they caused us some problems afterward because they said it was their livelihood, smuggling people, and we had stopped their livelihood. We busted the main ring leaders in 2009, and that's under control. But we had our lives threatened. There's no real protection when that happens. You can either lock yourself away and be scared, or you keep doing what you're doing.

If fishing was a drug, I'd be in trouble. I fish every chance I get. I've pretty much figured out the places to go. Everything has a season. Everything has a tide. And if you take notes, you can figure it out.

I like to keep my fishing places to myself because that's my shrink. My church. My sanity, pretty much. It's how I deal with a lot of things you have to deal with in these jobs. When you stay in one place you get to know people, and you get used to the wildlife. You start naming crocodiles and manatees. You start getting attached. And then you see a person you've been working with for fifteen years die, or a manatee gets hit by a powerboat.

Day in, day out, one of the hardest things about this job is dealing with different personalities, knowing everybody's problems. I tend to carry everybody's problems around with me. I want to help. In the summer it's easy 'cause there's not a lot of people around. But every year, in the winter, everybody comes back, and they remember the one Black guy that's been here forever, "Where is he? I want to talk to him." I know hundreds of people and know their life stories, and I carry it all around with me. And the guys that we didn't find on some of these search and rescues, some of the moms still call "to see how you're doing." And it reminds you over and over again about that person you didn't find.

I can think of three we never found. This one guy walked out of the campground before supper, older guy from out of town. Disappeared. We found Crocs, you know, the shoes that you wear, and didn't find the rest of him.

But being on the water—I don't have to catch fish all that much—it helps. It kind of relaxes me.

And most of the time we are able to help, able to rescue. A couple of years ago this gentleman was on a boat up in Ponce de Leon Bay with his wife, and while he was messing around on the sailboat, he fell and hit his head. He was confused, and then he passed out. Later, he woke up, but he wasn't alert enough to help his wife get him in safe condition. Another ranger and I, Rich Faner, responded to that one. We went out from Flamingo, headed up to Ponce de Leon Bay, a forty-five-minute run going as fast as you can. Once we got there, we saw the boat floundering in rough water. When we finally got onto his boat, he was down in the very bottom of the thirty-three foot sailboat.

Coast Guard boats arrived, but they were too big to get where we were, so they brought a helicopter in, and we dragged him to the top deck. But there was this big mast in the middle of the boat so the helicopter couldn't hover over us. They dropped a diver, and he swam to the boat. Meanwhile, I was trying to keep the guy stable, had high-flow oxygen on him. We got him on the backboard, put him on the front of my patrol boat, and from there they lifted him to the helicopter. He suffered brain damage, but with us getting there fast and putting high-flow oxygen on him, he was able to recuperate. He's sailing again.

There's a local guy that fishes in Flamingo just about every week. He has a medical condition, but he's fine most of the time. He went out poling, like many fishermen do, and he had an attack, and we couldn't get to him 'cause he was far out on the flats. It was too shallow, and the tide was still going out. The Coast Guard flew out a helicopter and the diver jumped, but there's only six inches of water so now he's stuck in the mud, trying to get to this guy. They pulled the diver back up and got him a little closer to the kid where he could pull himself out of the mud and onto the boat. Then they grabbed the kid and flew into Flamingo where we could start giving medical treatment out of our ambulance. He was having an attack that high-flow oxygen would basically take care of.

You know, most of the rescue incidents are things that people couldn't have planned for. Like that kid, the only way he can avoid having those problems is to stay at home and never have any fun. And the guy that was on the sailboat, I mean, all of us make those mistakes in life. And there's the fact that we wait till we get older and try to do the things that we've worked for all our life. We've saved the money to buy the sailboat when we retire. Okay, maybe you're really too old to be sailing then, but you can't tell somebody not to go sailing when they've been saving up to do it all their life. I mean, I deal with people that are enjoying life.

Getting out in the kayak and getting alone in the natural world to settle my mind, that didn't happen until I got married. My wife taught me that. Getting away.

Growing up, there was eleven of us, and there wasn't any alone time. My family are farmers, so it was sunup to sundown outside. But on the farm, I did have an old washing machine. I took the machine parts and threw them away and filled the tub with every ant family that I could find. I threw them into that tub, and I put diesel fuel under each leg so they couldn't get off of the washing machine. The washing machine was their whole world.

I took the glass part off an old screen door and set it on top, and I would look through the glass into the washing machine for hours, staring at the ants, watching them rebuild their ant populations. I would feed them cornbread and pinto beans, whatever my mom could afford to cook for us. That was the only time I got away. The only alone time I had was with the ants.

My wife taught me how to take advantage of fishing to be alone. She went with me a lot, but she didn't go with me all the time because she knew that that was my time. We've been married for twenty-three years, and we do a lot together, but she also pushes me to do things alone. She's my best friend. She's my buddy.

And the thing about mangrove fishing is it's just me, my kayak, and the mangroves out there. I can clear my thoughts up. I don't have to catch anything. When you get down in that kayak, you're a little lower, and you can see into the mangroves. You can get right up on stuff in a kayak. Alligators. Manatees. The manatees will let you come right up on 'em. And on a kayak, you can fish right by a flat where the birds feed.

When you're in civilization, if you got a problem, you can walk out of your house and go talk to somebody. Out in Mother Nature, you actually gotta think. There's nobody to talk to except the person you brought with you. If you take confusion out into the backcountry, you can come up with your own solution for what you're dealing with. That's what I do for myself on a weekly basis.

Of course, some people do go out there and take their boom boxes and all this stuff, set up camp. I used to do it too. And a lot of it, look at their age, it's a mating ritual. Just like the plumage on a bird is mating ritual. If there's a mixture of young male and female, whatever that guy can bring to distinguish himself from the rest of the males, he will bring.

And when men get together, we mark each other. We basically raise our leg and say, see, I did better than you. My fishing reel is better, or my kayak is faster. My grill cooks better than yours. The boom box, the colorful grill, the nice car, it's all plumage, just like a bird. When I'm writing tickets, I'm writing the ticket and thinking, "Your plumage is too much, buddy." Your loud radio, nope, can't do that. You cut a tree to set all this stuff up, so there's a resource violation. Your boat is way overpowered than what this plate says on your boat. Bad plumage. I mean, plumage gets a lot of people in trouble.

Once I was out on Cape Sable and saw this guy. I was going to write him a ticket for disturbance of natural features. I was younger, and I had a stereotype.

It was part of my survival. If this guy has long hair and a shaggy beard, he's probably a redneck, and he's not going to deal with me very well. I'll write this ticket, just hand it to him, tell him what he's done wrong, and not have to spend much time with him. So I ran the numbers on his boat, and it came back with his name, I put that down. All I had to do was ask him his phone number.

Then I pulled up to him. He has this anchor line tied to a beach naupaka tree (see photo on the right). I know what that is now, but I didn't then. He was in his boat, and he was horsin' it, *bbbbrrrrrrrrrrrrrrrrrr* . . . trying to pull that tree off the beach. I thought, "Dumb ass, man! God, that's a dumb guy." So I pulled up to him, and I said, "Stop what you're doing, right now."

He looked at me, and he says, "Do you know who I am?" or something like that, and I said, "No, I really don't care."

He says, "I'm Roger Hammer."

I said, "That's what your driver's license says." Then he started talking to me about the plant. That's what got me. He told me what it was and it was an exotic plant. I happened to be working Brazilian pepper at that time, spraying Brazilian pepper in Flamingo, so we sprung a conversation about exotic plants. I didn't tell him that I had already wrote the ticket, called it up to dispatch, and if he gave me any hell I was going to arrest him. He went on explaining to me about beach naupaka, and I'm like, "Okay. But don't ever tie up to another tree again. It looks really bad." Yeah. That looked really bad. I don't know how he came up with that, but it *was* a good solution to get that tree off the beach. Tying it to his boat and yanking it off.

*Beach Naupaka (*Scaevola tacada*). Roger Hammer explains that this plant is native to Indian and Pacific Ocean areas. In Florida, it is invasive. The invader is easily confused with native Inkberry (*Scaevola plumieri*). Photograph by Roger Hammer.*

We see him out there all the time. He usually looks like he's overpacked when he leaves out of the marina, but he goes offshore and catches big fish. And he does these crazy camping trips all the way up to the middle of the park. He knows us. He can say, "Hey, Tony, if I'm not at Willy Willy by so and so, come check on me." But he's still got a lot of plumage.

The original Flamingo ranger station was at Coot Bay, but they moved the station and the ranger residence area closer to the water. Basically, they cut the new residence area in the middle of the mangrove forest.

Early September, the rattlesnakes start. You know how a female dog goes into heat and all the males follow her. Rattlesnakes do kind of the same thing. Late August it starts, runs into September. And every year those rattlesnakes show up in the mangrove area like they always did, only it's a housing area now. I have to catch 'em and take 'em out of people's basements, get them out of the shop. But in 2013, they were fatter, a little more aggressive. I was in town and got a call, "Tony, there's a rattlesnake in the kayak room where we keep the paddles. The researchers can't get in there."

So I drove down the road, frustrated, because I'd had to come all the way from town, and I got my snake bag and went in there and grabbed the snake, five and a half feet long. I'm putting her in the bag, and I hear *sssssssss*. . . . "Oh, shit, there's another one." It took my mind off the one I had in my hand, and I dropped it without letting it get all the way in the bag. She grabbed me. Her whole weight and one fang grabbed me on the fingertip.

I watched venom run down my hand. Her head started doing that little curl thing; she was digging in deeper. I grabbed her back of the head and dropped her in the bag, went out and called my buddy from Miami-Dade. "I just got bit by a rattlesnake."

"Tony. This ain't time to be joking."

"It's a diamondback. I need antivenin."

"Oh, shit. Just head to Homestead Hospital."

One of my employees drove me up the road, and a helicopter met me at Mahogany Hammock and took me to the hospital. They pushed me down on a stretcher, and a nurse kept telling me, "Tony, you need to breathe, you need to breathe." I'm like, "I'm breathing." But I wasn't talking. I was out.

My heart stopped. Obviously, I don't remember this part, but they gave me a shot to get my heart back running. When they finally got the antivenin and gave me a shot, it didn't work. After thirteen doses of antivenin, it started reversing the feeling of a hot iron beating on my hand. Every time my heart beat, that iron would hit my hand. That was some crazy ass pain.

The next day, the doctor came in and said, "Your hand is compartmentalized, and we need to cut your finger off. If we don't, the rot in your finger is going to cause you to lose your whole arm."

I said, "You're not cutting on me."

He said, "Well, if you don't, you're going to lose your hand."

I said, "Sir, as long as I can touch the tip of my finger and it turns red again, I'm holding onto my finger, 'cause that would be my job."

He said, "Alright. Sign a waiver."

That little tip of the finger was still alive, so I held onto hope. My arm started getting a little reddish underneath, and two days later it turned black. I thought, "Maybe that doctor is right."

Again, he wanted to cut it off. I said, "I'm in law enforcement. In law enforcement, we want to arrest people. You're a doctor, and you want to have surgery. I know you're in a hurry, but I'm going to wait." As long as I could touch that little tip of my finger and it got pink, I'm like, "Man, there's still circulation there. I'm not cutting that finger off." And it started coming back around.

If you were a religious person, you might say that it was meant for me to get bit. Because two weeks after that bite, they were going to get rid of Miami-Dade's antivenin/poison control unit. It's basically a helicopter, $320,000 a year in the budget. They were going to get rid of it. When I had just got out of the hospital, this lady says, "Tony. I know you're in pain. I know you're not recovered from the bite. But everybody knows who you are. We need you to be on TV." So I got my sick butt out of bed and they put me on the news. And Dan Kimball, park superintendent, he called Washington, and they put pressure on Miami-Dade. So they kept the unit. Something good happened. From my stupidity. Picking that snake up and not paying attention to what I was doing.

It's not allowed to take lobster from the park. The lobsters use the park, the mangrove roots, and the flats to protect their young while they're small. If you look into the mangroves, you see the small snook, small redfish, small lobsters. They stay in those mangrove roots until they can protect themselves and move fast enough to get away from predators. Without the park, there'd be a lot less lobsters around here, definitely. But pretty much every week in summer we catch people poaching lobsters from the park.

You know, I have to put a life force on everything so I can appreciate it. And the life force of the mangroves is that they want to grow. They are reaching out and just continually spreading, dropping more of their little wings, and spreading out over the Everglades. It's amazing. You can go back to a spot in just one year, and you can

Snowy egret on old mangrove. Note the yellow feet characteristic of this bird. Sometimes a snowy egret dangles her "golden slippers" in water to attract fish. Photograph by Anne McCrary Sullivan.

tell that that's a good mangrove there, it's got some good will to grow. A path that I used to go through fishing is closed in, darn it. So I just stop at the mangrove.

The mangroves have protected the Everglades from development. The mangroves basically kicked Henry Flagler's butt. Flagler's idea was building a bridge from Cape Sable to Key West. If you read those old books about him trying to get

workers to clear roads and stuff, the mangrove forest and mosquitoes kept them away from here.

The Model Land Company guys really wanted to develop this area too. They probably would've, but the people that came and looked at it said, "I'm not investing my money in that." So, you know, the mangroves do a good job. They take care of

themselves and take care of the park. If we let them do what they're designed to do, they'll be protecting this place for a long time.

Katrina would have tore this place apart, Hurricane Wilma, too, if it wasn't for the mangroves protecting the shore-line. Their root system is entwined with the soil, and it's a tight system. The hurricane pushes all this water in, and when it's going back out, the good stuff doesn't go back out with it because the mangroves are protecting what's there. We wouldn't have a park without the mangroves.

The Everglades and the mangrove forest are still evolving. I'm seeing a lot more mangrove islands popping up in the bays I'm patrolling. In areas of Florida Bay and in the backcountry, the mangroves are making more land in the Everglades. Besides that, I see more fish populations in the mangrove roots when I'm paddling through them on Florida Bay. I see how the mangroves make a lit-tle day care for baby redfish, small snook, little lobsters, until they get big enough to be on their own. I'm a law enforce-ment guy. It's all about protection.

Osprey with chick. Photograph by Anne McCrary Sullivan.

REACHING INTO THE MANGROVE MUCK

Susan Reece

SUPERVISORY PARK RANGER, EVERGLADES NATIONAL PARK

When I first came to the Everglades as a seasonal ranger in Flamingo, I fell in love with this place. Paddling, watching the birds go in and out from rookeries. I just found this place unbelievable. My seasonal job ended after five months and I went away for a while. Then I said, "I've got to get back to the Everglades." I applied and came back and said, "I could spend my whole life here and never learn it all." It's been twenty years. This has been a great job and, ignoring the government bureaucracy, it's just . . . look where I get to live and work!

In my office at Gulf Coast, I look out the window at ibises sitting in mangrove trees, pelicans flying over. The mangroves are the heart of it. They hold this whole place together. Mangroves start the whole food web by dropping leaves into the water, into the muck, and then leaves are fed on by algae and bacteria. Eventually the leaves break down, fall apart, become this nice detritus soup that's fed on by the smaller organisms, working their way up to little crabs and shrimp, and then the fish, who feed the birds and dolphins, sharks, everything else.

I wish I could be outside all the time, in wildlife, in nature, even when it's all mosquitoey. That's why I became a park ranger, to be part of nature. And I love sharing it with visitors, so, in a way, I like it when I'm short-staffed and can be working the visitor center desk. I love to see visitors when they're excited about things, even something we may see and hear every day.

Local fishermen use the mangrove backcountry all the time, so we have lots of conversations with them. We talk to some of the business owners in Everglades City, but less so. When I first came here, I remember a local business owner talking about the area and how much he loved it, his family, generations living here. And listening to him I was like, "That's fantastic." Then he went into how the Park Service ruined everything and, "You people. You people." I said, "Well, remember, Congress established this park in 1934, so that was well before any of our people were here." I asked him, "What do you think would have happened to the area if the park hadn't been established?"

At first I could see he was going to say, "Well, I still could do whatever I want," but he stopped and he thought about it—I listened to him, he listened to me—and he goes, "It'd probably look like Miami."

And I go, "Yeah, that's kind of what I think."

We help paddlers set up their itineraries all the time, either by phone or when they walk in. Now, if somebody comes in and it's clear that they are ill-prepared, we warn them. We won't deny somebody a permit, but we will try to get them to do something within their means. And we play off each other. From my office I can hear conversations at the desk, and if I hear the ranger trying to be nice about it, and I'm looking at the time, it's 3:30, there's twenty knot winds, and they're going *where*? And there's three hours of daylight? I just walk through, as a pass-through like I know nothing, and I'm like, "Oh, my, you're late for a permit. Where're you going?" And then, "Oh, you're never going to get *there*," and I just keep right on walking. I've trained my staff, if it's a group of people, look at the one who's worried. Say, "This is really not recommended. This could be a life and death situation and you really should wait a day. Or you could do this shorter trip." We try to find ways to discourage them from putting themselves in danger. We don't want anyone hurt.

We also don't want them just to get across to Sandfly Island and say, "We're stopping here." That's not a campsite. And we don't want a call-out at 10:00 at night because they swamped their canoe and they're not anywhere near a campsite. Law enforcement is called out and they're annoyed with us, "Why did you write them a permit?" And we say, "We can't not do it." We do our best to stop it. We read the rules and regs aloud. We ask them if they've seen the trip planner. How many times can we tell them these things? It's frustrating, you know, when they come back and say, "You didn't tell us."

You know, you're here many years and you start noticing patterns. Like watching adult pelicans teaching the young pelicans. That was something I didn't realize right away. I would see an adult pelican flying along with two or three young ones behind, and it would turn and dive into the water, the next one would turn and dive, the next one, next one, and they weren't going after anything. It was like they were just practicing how to turn and dive. They would fly up again, not too high above the water and do it again, march their way across Chokoloskee Bay doing this kind of synchronized flight and dive. It was always the young ones following the adult, and it was like the parent was saying, "Let me show you how to turn, plunge into the water, come back up." It was so cool to see that.

And there's a big rookery nearby. Pelicans are nesting in there. And cormorants, herons, egrets. And right here at the Visitor Center we have the white ibis, sitting in branches, turkey vultures flying overhead. When the wind comes in, especially a storm from the west or southwest, the magnificent frigatebirds will be flying over-head. Always exciting to see that.

I remember when I first came to Gulf Coast for a permanent job. We were on a boat tour, out by Indian Key Pass. We were watching dolphins for quite a while, and then I asked the captain, "What's in that little mangrove island?" He kind of moves as close as he dares, we're both looking, and I'm like, "Oh, my god, it's frigatebirds!" And they were sitting in trees. I'd never seen that. I remember going to Dry Tortugas and waiting three days for one to land. I never saw it.

So I get on the mic, and I go, "If anyone's interested, there are magnificent frigatebirds actually sitting in the trees," and this woman turns around and says, "We really don't care." I was devastated. We come back in and my supervisor asks, "How was your boat tour?" I said, "Oh, it was okay," kind of nonchalant. I said, "We did see a couple of frigatebirds sitting in a tree." She goes, "Oh, my god, I've never seen them sitting in a tree!" That had been my reaction and the boat captain's reaction, but then, "We really don't care."

But then I realized that these people probably didn't even know what the birds were. And I'm calling them "magnificent," you know. That's their name, but per-haps people didn't know that. I learned that if I wanted to impress people who aren't birders, I just say it's a birder's bird. It was a big deal, you know, to see like a Caspian tern. Nobody would care, and then I would say, "Oh, birders would be going nuts over that one." But yeah, the bird life associated with the mangroves is awesome.

This estuary has two high tides and two low tides a day, really cool. I love to watch the tide move, and the wading birds move with it. We sometimes have spoonbills right here on the mudflats by the Visitor Center. Snowy egrets and great blue herons follow them, taking advantage of the spoonbill's swinging back and forth, scaring up fish. It's awesome.

The osprey nest (see photo on page 30) right out front on the channel marker is fun to watch. It can be kind of depressing in the spring, though, when sometimes the young ones take their first flight and don't have enough strength to get back to

The world of the western Everglades is a world of water, clouds, and reflections. Photograph by Holly Genzen.

the marker, end up in the water. You know, you want to let nature take its course, but you can't sit there and watch a bird drown after all that struggle all winter and spring to get to that point. So, yeah, we'll go and pick it up. Usually we can't get it back on the channel marker, but we take it to the island right there in front, stick it on the island. And the parents usually come back and take care of it.

Seasonal changes here are definitely subtle, but when you've been here a while, you start noticing. One of the first signs of fall is when the kingfishers return, usually at the end of August. We get excited because, "Oh, it *is* going to get cooler. Summer rains *will* stop. Winter is coming."

One of the first signs of spring is the arrival of the swallow-tailed kites. It's kind

Mud and mangrove roots.
Photograph by Holly Genzen.

of a game for us. Who's going to see one before the end of February as they come up from South America. It's like, "Ah! A sign of spring. We saw the first swallow-tailed kite today." Then in March, we see white pelicans gathering, and suddenly it seems like all the white pelicans from Flamingo are at Gulf Coast getting ready for migration.

Summer months, the water levels are higher. Part of that is seasonal rains, but we also have more winds blowing from the south and south-southwest, blowing water in, so tides are higher.

In summer, the water seems calmer, and you can see everything in the water, from jellyfish to tiny baby rays swimming along. And we notice the sharks coming in, even into the marina, and that's always kind of exciting.

Also, when the water heats up, blue-green algae break off at the bottom and rise to the surface, more oxygen dissolving. We call it "the rising of the scum." And in summer we see lots of red mangrove propagules floating, big mats of them. It's easy to say we have only a wet season and a dry season, you know, summer and winter, but there are definitely spring and fall.

People go, "Oh, your trees don't lose their leaves." Well, yeah, the trees lose their leaves, but mangroves drop only a small percentage of their leaves at a time, and that's part of how the food chain works. In March, the mahoganies suddenly turn brown and drop all their leaves at once, but then a week later they're fully green again, and you're like, that was the fastest fall-to-spring ever. The same thing with the sea grapes. You say, "Wait a minute. The leaves are all turning orange and red. The ground is littered with them." And then they're bright green again. It happens so fast. Gumbo limbo will lose their leaves sometimes in the winter months, depending how dry it is, then green up in the spring.

One of my favorite things, when I do canoe trips out there, is landing on an oyster bar or a mangrove island, reaching into the mangrove muck. I love the smell of mangrove muck, especially where it doesn't get a lot of tidal change, the water kind of sits. Then if you go disturb that area, whether it's with a canoe paddle or if you try to walk through, you release all that hydrogen sulfide gas, that rotten egg smell. It's like the smell of death and the smell of new life all at once. It's amazing stuff, you know, the leaves and other organisms dying, starting the whole new food chain. I love the mangrove estuary. I love that smell.

MOUNDS OF THE TEN THOUSAND ISLANDS

Margo Schwadron

ARCHAEOLOGIST, NATIONAL PARK SERVICE

One of the first people to study the area was C. B. Moore from 1900 to 1905. He was looking for treasure, big pots and gold and all that good stuff, and he wrote off the Ten Thousand Islands, said, "It's really of no interest" because as much digging around as he did, he just found shells.

But he was impressed with the architecture, impressed with Chokoloskee, the largest of all of the sites. His descriptions said there were two huge mounds on either side of the island, fifty feet tall, and they were flat-topped. They had remains of fire pits at the tops, and there were canals and depressions, water courts, all the features we see preserved on other sites.

One has to wonder about the position of Chokoloskee, its relationship with the other sites. This one was the largest. What we see archaeologically with clusters of sites is what we would see in our modern world—a capital city, one which maybe was a political center or a ceremonial center.

Unfortunately, we will never know. It's been developed now. But we do have old aerial photos and some older maps. At the southwest part of the island there's a large house with a big landholding, and if you drive over there you can see the terrain, how it's undulating. It's all shell midden underneath.

THE TURNER RIVER SITE

Ales Hrdlicka visited the Turner River site in 1919. Hrdlicka was a famous anthropologist with the Smithsonian who, in 1910, published *Anthropology of Florida* with his visual interpretation of the site, rows of mounds, Chokoloskee and Turner River really close to one another. He notes that there's one outer row of mounds and then another row that are more round and more elongated. And there's a plaza-like area.

Mangroves were part of the ecosystem in prehistoric times, and I would guess mangroves fronted the shoreline just like they do today. With all that mangrove in front, you would need some sort of way to land, to bring your canoe in. I'm not surprised that they engineered their sites to allow the water to flow in. Water was a central part of their existence and their cosmology. Not only would canals make an easy way to bring your canoes in, they would make it easy to capture fish during high tide—throw a net down, and as the tide is going out, capture those fish. The key is that this is purposeful, not just random. Some people argue, because it is shell midden, it is garbage, just a place where they are disposing of shells. But this is different. This is a different example in the world of how they're consciously shaping their settlement *with* their garbage.

The mounds aren't 100 percent oyster. It's probably like 95 percent oyster. We find species of whelk—left-handed lightning whelks, crown conchs—other bivalves, sometimes clams. And there are fish remains. There's some midden material in here which suggests that this isn't an exclusive oyster-harvesting site. People were definitely living here. We find pottery. It was definitely a village, but they were exploiting a lot of oysters. So everything you see there today, even though it's covered with leaves, it's all shell. And at the bottom of this we're finding muck, like a marine origin muck as if the site was built in the water.

One of the challenges we have in interpreting this site is, why do you have this

Margo Schwadron holds an image of the Turner River Shell Company map. Photograph by Anne McCrary Sullivan.

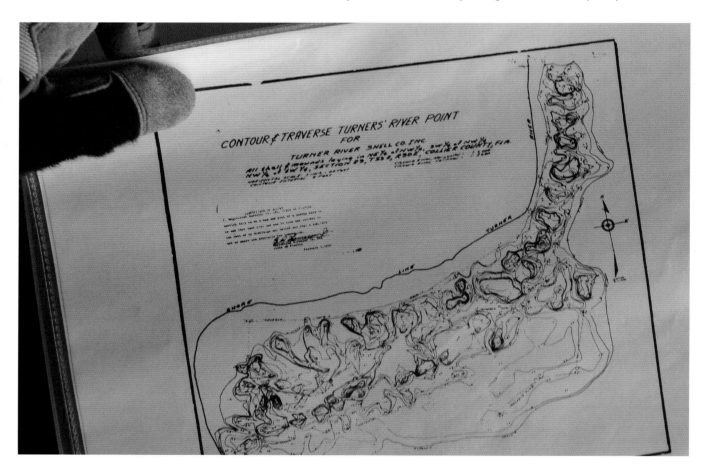

little, tiny depression in between the mounds? Would this have been a house site, like a longhouse built on stilts? And then, when they're just sitting and munching and eating their oysters, they're throwing it to the left, throwing it to the right. One hundred, two hundred years later there is just a negative depression for where the house was? That's a possibility. Or were they building these up and living on top of them? Who knows? I'm guessing they had longhouses just because the mounds are long, and it would have been hard to put a round thing on it. It's a house style that works in the tropics, elevated. You get up a little bit higher, there's less bugs, less mosquitoes, more wind.

You know, it may be that the house platform was there, and they made a conscious decision, instead of throwing their garbage all over the place, "Just keep putting it in front of you and we'll build it out and build it out, and, hey, that makes a nice place where we can walk and stay up high out of the bugs." The mounds at Turner River are very narrow and really peaked. That shape would suggest that things were being dropped from on top. Like, if you had a basket of shells, would you hike up the side of a hill to dump it?

There's a set of mounds that are sort of different shaped, more conical. What we found by testing and radiocarbon dating was that this was the earliest part of the site. We did radiocarbon dates on the top and radiocarbon dates on the bottom, and they were like, fifty years apart. So it means these were built very rapidly, probably within a hundred years.

We have a lot of pottery from the Turner River site. They're all fired. A lot of them are decorated, and that's one of the reasons we know they're different from the folks further north in Calusa heartland. These simple styles are more prevalent down here. The decorations are usually simple incisions underneath the rim, ticking, sometimes dots, sometimes bigger hatches, sometimes a little chevron hatch that goes up and down. We usually find small fragments, but if we have enough of a rim, we can estimate the rim diameter, so we know the bowls are small and shallow.

In the 1950s, the Turner River site was owned by the Smallwood family. They began dredging and started hauling the shell away. There was an outcry, and somebody contacted the University of Florida and said, "This really important archaeological site down in the Everglades is getting destroyed." They got William Sears to come down and do an investigation. Ripley Bullen and other archaeologists at the Florida Museum of Natural History came down for a site visit. Bullen tried to map it, but it was so complicated, he just kind of gave up. The first topographic map was the survey map (see photo on page 40) that the Smallwood family and their Turner River Shell Company had done in order to estimate how much shell was there so they

could get a dollar value for it when the National Park Service was acquiring property.

Now we have LIDAR. It's basically flown by aircraft, giving very accurate scans. Someone has to work to extract all the trees out of the scan, extract it to bare earth, but we now have a much more accurate map of what the settlement looked like based on the LIDAR mapping. We can see that these mounds are huge. Imagine twenty-five feet tall, one hundred feet long. Some are more massive than others, but all in a row. And it looks like depressions in between them that probably would have been the canals.

I love this Turner River site. It's incredible, and we're so lucky to have it. I think a great story in all this is the movement to preserve it in the fifties. We've lost so many sites in Florida, especially on the east coast, for road fill. Turtle Mound's another one where all the mounds around it were destroyed, and a group of people at the turn of the century were avid to protect it. They saved it.

Mangrove roots in shell.
Photograph by Holly Genzen.

SHELL RING SITES

The "shell rings" are among our earliest archaeological sites in the Ten Thousand Islands. They go back thousands of years into the Archaic period. Horr's Island is a shell ring, and Russell Key. Sandfly Key is also a series of rings. These are totally manmade, anthropogenic, built by prehistoric people. All oyster shells.

The shell rings aren't closed circles. We don't really see those down here, but we do see an abandonment of one ring and then establishment of a bigger ring. We see that over and over again. Maybe the original site was shifting. Maybe sea level was changing, and they needed to move their site. There could be religious reasons. Perhaps they've had people die, and they've decided, "We're not going to live on our cemetery anymore. It's time to move on." We do see at a lot of sites, there are burials on the earlier parts, and it becomes like a sacred area, separated by water and mangroves.

Central depressions, we call them "water courts," probably were to store fish, an analog to agriculture when people are sedentary in an area and they need to have a backup food supply. They could have been for freshwater storage, too, sites where they were digging down to tap into an artesian well, bring up fresh water. Or they could be fish weirs. Groups could go and cast a big net out there during a tide, capture a lot of fish.

People didn't just go out in the middle of the water and start a settlement. There may have been a little sand flat or an oyster shoal. They started extracting oysters, dumping the shells, extracting oysters, dumping shells, over and over, and land started to build, and "Oh, hey, let's keep coming back to this spot. We can put a little camp here; we've got some land." I would argue against them having this end product in mind when they started.

Dismal Key, Fakahatchee Key, Sandfly Key, Russell Key, these are the latest, and they were all abandoned about 1300 CE, all at the same time. That's kind of a mystery. Something changed, whether it was a cultural thing or some external factor, maybe a new threat or new competition for resources, maybe sea level change. Maybe they had simply overexploited an area. We do know a little Ice Age was happening right around this time. Or maybe their population just got too big.

A lot of people call this whole southwestern coast "Calusa area." I've always argued against that. You have the Ten Thousand Islands and then going north, from about Cape Romano or Key Marco, the shoreline is just beach. There's no inner mangroves until you get up to Charlotte Harbor—and that's the Calusa area. There's a distinct geographic boundary, like a natural zone of no occupation. Whereas here, south of Cape Romano and Key Marco, you see a pattern, like it's every quarter mile, and the sites look the same and they all date to the same time period.

There's no doubt the groups interacted with one another. And what I think is that the Calusa became so powerful and dominant that they had an influence over all of South Florida. A lot of protohistoric records say that all of South Florida had to pay tribute up to the Calusa to keep from warring. We see, archaeologically, some distinct ceramic forms in the Calusa area that we see rarely down here. But some decorated types from here, we see up there, which to me says the flow of exchange is going that way. It's tribute. There may be things coming back, but it doesn't appear to be ceramics. It really looks like there's two different groups. So I would shy away from calling them all Calusa. People have been referencing "Glades Culture" down here for years, and that works. I would say, "People of the Ten Thousand Islands." The

Ten Thousand Islands is defined geologically from the Key Marco/Cape Romano area all the way down the mangrove coast to Flamingo.

When Hurricane Wilma made a direct hit in 2005, I volunteered to come down and do a hurricane damage assessment. We would go out to the sites, walk over them, and document any erosion or damage that has happened. It was a pretty rough hit. I worked in an incident command team with a whole bunch of law enforcement rangers. We knew there was a big storm surge and before we went out, we did a little predictive model of which sites probably got hit the worst. We went to every single one of them.

That was the first time I stepped foot on them. I took a lot of notes and photographed, and it sparked this desire, like, "We've got to do something to get these documented. They're just incredible."

Soon after that I decided to go on for my PhD, do a dissertation that would document these sites. I thought, they're listed now as National Register sites, but they should be National Historic Landmark sites. We'll need more data to support that. I worked with the park and the park came up with some funding and some seed money for about two years. At the same time, National Geographic gave me a Young Explorer grant to look at Dismal Key and Fakahatchee Key, which are outside the park. I did fieldwork from early 2006 up to 2008 or 2009 and then wrote the dissertation.

I've always been concerned about climate change and sea level rise. Even back in 1997 when I worked for the State of Florida, we looked at predicting sea level rise and the potential impact on archaeological sites that are most vulnerable. Now the Park Service is really concerned. So we're going to study the sites that are more in the southern Ten Thousand Islands, like Hamilton Mound and Johnson Mound. Because, you know, in fifty or one hundred years, these sites are going to be under water.

We're doing a long-term work now to try to get these sites nominated as National Historic Landmarks. Ultimately, I would argue for World Heritage designation. There's no example like this anywhere else in the world. There are other examples of really large shell mounds, like Brazil's Sambaquis, which are huge, but they don't have this kind of elaboration and this pattern, using the shell as a form of architecture.

Manatee surfacing in seagrass in Florida Bay. Photograph by Anne McCrary Sullivan.

MANATEES, DOLPHINS, PYTHONS, AND BATS

Skip Snow

WILDLIFE BIOLOGIST, EVERGLADES NATIONAL PARK

They named the manatee Linda. I have a picture of her, and me with her, in water almost up to my neck. The US Fish and Wildlife Service and the Florida State Fish and Game had a program, and they may still have it, to try and introduce into the wild manatees that were basically taking up bed space in the different seaquaria—Lowry Park over in Tampa, Sea World in Orlando, and Miami Seaquarium. There are some in other states, too, that can hold and rehabilitate manatees, whether they're injured in the wild or abandoned calves or the mom died, or they don't know what. These captive manatees have no experience in the wild, and they're taking up space, not contributing to the population's recovery as an endangered species. What do you do? A group of different agencies and nongovernmental organizations developed a program to introduce the manatees into the wild.

They had to teach the manatees to socialize. So they started by putting them in tanks with others. They also had to teach them how to feed because all the feeding in captivity goes on at the surface, but that's not where manatees normally feed, right? They normally feed on submerged vegetation. So they came up with these mechanisms to hold lettuce, things that sank to the bottom, so the manatees would go down. All kinds of different stuff they did to try and train them, and when they felt that they were healthy and acclimated to other animals, we needed to release them. And where do we do that?

For a while, in the late 1990s and early 2000s, there were releases into our wild population in Everglades National Park. These releases usually took place in Whitewater Bay out of Flamingo. All of the released animals had a radio tag so they could be tracked and postrelease assessments done. We would either fly and look for them or we would go by boat to get a visual on them, see how they were doing and if they were with other animals. Just check up on them to see how they were adjusting to the wild. There were a number of animals released over the years. One of those was Linda. Linda was released and her movements followed.

Manatees are explorers. They like to go up creeks and into tight places. The Buckleys named a lot of those little places with local names like Pickle Lake, different little places that manatees like to go. We noticed from her radio tag that Linda had been spending a lot of time in some little backwater off the North River. She hadn't been leaving, so we were concerned. First thing we did was go check and see that the tag was still on the manatee, 'cause sometimes the tags break off. They are designed to do that so the manatee doesn't get stranded.

And the manatees have no neck, right? And no waist. They don't have anything convenient for attaching something except right before it gets to the big peduncle, the big tail. There's a narrowing there, and that's where they put a belt and then attach this long tether. The tether has a weak link in it so that if it gets hung up in debris or hit by something, it breaks off and the manatee doesn't get entangled.

So anyway, we went out to check on Linda, way up this little creek. We got the signal, but it wasn't actually in the creek. It was on the other side of a very low, scrubby mangrove area, a tangle of mangrove roots. We could see water on the other side but there was no way in.

We looked at maps, we looked on the water, we couldn't figure out exactly how she got into this small mangrove lake. There was no way in that we could see. So we tied up the boat and then literally walked our way over the mangrove peat and mangrove roots, maybe fifty yards, to get into the lake to check on her. Sure enough, there she was, cruising around, and the tag was still attached.

Then we looked around to do an assessment of what was there for her to eat. We saw hardly any submerged aquatic vegetation, and there wasn't a lot of anything else she might use as a food source. We decided to supplement her efforts, which meant going back, building a floating square, a couple of meters by a couple of meters of PVC tube. Then I would stop by Publix and see if they would give me a box of romaine, 'cause that's what manatees like, they like the expensive stuff. And you can't give them just a little bit. They eat a lot.

So we piled the box of romaine and the PVC pipes into a boat, went out there, hiked across the fifty yards of mangrove root and peat, assembled the tubes and filled the floating corral with romaine. We then tethered it to some mangroves.

Once or twice a week we would go back and feed and see what she was doing. She was eating but not as well as the vets would like her to. And she was still there. She didn't leave. We looked more, from the water and also from satellite images, trying to find out how she got in. We could not and still to this day don't know how unless maybe there was a very high tide that she got up on and she could swim or sort of struggle over the mangrove roots.

There was concern because she was eating, but not well. The decision was made to get her out. We thought we could get a bunch of people to corral her onto a stretcher and then, all of us, haul her over that sort of scrubby mangrove area to deeper water. But it was deemed that we couldn't possibly carry all that weight, no matter how many people we had. So we decided to use a helicopter to lift her out and over to a boat.

So I worked with our aviation specialist at the time, Gary Carnel, and we figured out the logistics of getting a bunch of people out there to get Linda into the stretcher. We also dragged a canoe across the mangrove roots into that little pond so that somebody could be more mobile because it's pretty deep, and it was mucky, hard to move around. So the person in the canoe helped herd the manatee towards us. On the other side of the mangrove ring, we had boats waiting, and we had a helicopter.

Then we corralled her with a net, and at the very last minute she swam right into the stretcher, a floating stretcher made specifically for transporting manatees. We had hooks on it, had it all set up to be lifted by what they call a "long line" dangling from the bottom of the helicopter.

So the helicopter came down, we hooked the straps to the stretcher, and they lifted her over the mangroves that she obviously couldn't figure out how to get back out of. The helicopter then plunked her down on the back of a specially designed boat for hauling manatees. They unhooked her from the helicopter, and off she went on the boat. The rest of us had to trudge our way out and find our way back. It's amazing that it worked as well as it did and no one got hurt.

They took Linda back to one of the aquaria to get checked out. She was undernourished. Largely because of having not fed well for some period of time, she had lost the beneficial bacteria that were in her gut that helped her digest. She needed to be inoculated or reinoculated with her favorable gut flora. Either that didn't happen or it didn't take. I'm not sure. But either way, we would learn later that she had died. After all that effort, we were kind of upset about that. It was quite the struggle, and we were disappointed 'cause she was lively at the time we caught her. First time I've ever seen a flying manatee.

On the navigational charts, I like what they always write when it gets all gray and the lines marking water channels kind of disappear, they write in there, "Numerous ponds and streams." I just love it. 'Cause yeah, that's right! When you paddle through any of those, they're narrow and deep. It's quiet and nice, and here you

Sunset at Sweetwater Creek.
Photograph by
Anne McCrary Sullivan.

come paddling, and all of a sudden a manatee will just bolt underwater. They can be really fast for a short period of time. That displacement of a 1,500 pound animal quickly causes a hole in the water. Sometimes the water drops right underneath your boat or right before you, and it can be really unnerving. The bolt startles you, and then the water just vanishes.

You know who else encounters manatees? I've only seen this once, at Flamingo, behind the marina store. A bunch of us were looking out over the water in the Buttonwood Canal. There were manatees lolling about, not feeding, just surface resting. So here comes this alligator, no particular hurry, cruising along toward one of the manatees, and when he gets closer, he starts to climb on the manatee's back, I kid you not. Now, what's *that* about? Does the alligator know it's a manatee or just think it's something to haul itself out on? Darned if the alligator doesn't get most of the way up on the back of this manatee before the manatee, I guess, wakes up? Or maybe it knew the alligator was there and then just decided he didn't like it? I'm not sure, but the manatee had been calm and not responding until the alligator had a fair amount of itself out of the water and onto its back. Then both of them bolted. The manatee goes this way, and the alligator goes the opposite way. Big splash of water! And everybody is saying, "What was *that*?"

I first came to Everglades National Park in April 1988 as a backcountry manager, but after a couple of years, there was a need for personnel to do other kinds of ecological work. I became a wildlife ecologist, coordinated a project to restore the eastern bluebird and the brown-headed nuthatch to the park and the wild turkey to the pinelands. And then I got the additional duty of invasive animals.

Invasive animals came on my plate in a big way in 2003. There had been some Burmese pythons found, few and far between, but nonetheless troubling, as early as the mid-1990s. But in winter of 2003, an alligator and a python were found locked together in battle at the Anhinga Trail. It went on for at least twenty-four hours, probably more like thirty, and both animals seemed to survive and swim off and be gone. That was the management trigger to say, "Okay, Skip, take some time and see what kind of a problem we have." For the next decade, invasive animals in general, but specifically the Burmese pythons, kind of hijacked my career. It was challenging to find time to do other things, but I don't regret it. I guess it's not one of those things that you've orchestrated, it just came to you. Like ET, you know. *He came to me!* So, Burmese pythons came to me, and we spent the decade together.

The first Burmese pythons collected in the park were collected by the then museum curator, Walter Mishaka, a professional herpetologist. He found, I think, three pythons in that Hells Bay, West Lake area, where the mangroves and the prairie meet.

They're cryptic, very difficult to see, and hard to detect. They could have been here and breeding in the park back in the eighties, and we would just not know. For our purposes, the first ones were in the mid-1990s, and then in 2003 the number of animals we had evidence of, shot up dramatically. Until 2009. The winter of 2009–2010 was historically unprecedented. We've had freezes here before, but we've never had a week of temperatures in the forties and then a freeze. Lots of things suffered. We lost a lot of manatees and American crocodiles, and a significant number of Burmese pythons also succumbed. Not all of them. They're still here.

Oron "Sonny" Bass tells the story of the ivory-billed woodpecker crew that came out here trying to find remnant populations of ivory-billed. They looked at the old growth areas of mangroves, the really tall ones, like in the Shark River and the Harney, checking out snags. From one of the holes the crew was checking, out pops a

Wormvine orchid (Vanilla barbellata), Hells Bay Canoe Trail. Decimated by collectors, the endangered wormvine orchid has an almost leafless climbing stem. Its flowers have yellow-green petals with a purple-marked lip and appear in the summertime, opening in the night and closing by midday. Photograph by Anne McCrary Sullivan.

Burmese python. So there's a great picture of this Burmese python coming out of a hole, deep, deep in the mangroves, as far away from anywhere as you could get. So, yeah. They're there.

But are you likely to encounter them? I'd be a whole lot more concerned about weather. I'd be more concerned about reactions to insect bites and how you might react to those. I'd be concerned about your abilities or lack of abilities in choosing routes based upon tide and winds. I think those things are of greater risk to our visitors. I might be mildly concerned about alligators that people have fed or that have become habituated where fishermen have dumped their bait. Those concern me more than a Burmese python. The riskiest thing that a visitor to the park does is the drive from the airport to the park. Data wise, no question. But we're not rational that way.

I'm working now with the folks doing acoustic surveying for our bat populations in the park. I like it 'cause it has a Christmas component to it. Every time you go out, you have an inkling, but you don't really know what you're going to get.

I like to think that bats leak information. Through their calls they can tell us what species they are and whether they are feeding or socializing. We have an acoustic tool, a bat detector, that allows us to hear what they're doing. It records the call and transforms it so we can go back to the lab and we can hear it and analyze it on a computer. And there's this sort of Christmas morning endeavor of opening and, "What did I get? Oh, look at that!" It's a bit of a thrill.

Bats live in a world that we have difficulty being a part of. Our sensory ecology is so different from theirs. They use ultrasonic sound in a manner that we can't use or even detect, and they fly, and they do all this at night. There's a world of bats immersed in ours, and when we intersect, we don't know each other.

There's a bat out there called the Florida bonneted bat. Its name is *Eumops floridanus*. It is the largest bat in Florida now, also the rarest. It's endemic to South Florida, doesn't occur anywhere else in the world. We have detected these deep in the mangroves, at Darwin's Place and Watsons Place and just outside of the park at Dismal Key.

They're a big bat, and they have long narrow wings indicative of a bat that flies far, flies fast, flies high. They can go quite far in a night to feed and come back. So they could make use of habitat that provides roosts but is quite far from where their foraging happens. They roost, as far as we can tell, in barrel shapes and in tree cavities.

We have done repeated detections in the Flamingo area. Some seasons there's tremendous bat activity at the Buttonwood Bridge. Standing there, can't see a thing, and there's just all this stuff going on.

Historical figures have told good stories, like the Dimocks, A.W. and Julian, father and son, in the early 1900s. It was back in the time of the "gentleman explorer," and they wrote for magazines like *Travel and Leisure* or *Field and Stream*. They made a couple of trips down here, and one of their big trips was cruising, a sailboat carrying smaller skiffs. They cruised and camped, would drop anchor wherever they wanted and go off up the creeks and explore and write about that and take pictures, great pictures. The whole collection is now at the American Museum of Natural History in New York.

Some of the Dimocks' writings are captured in a book called *Florida Enchantments*. They describe in this great little bit of prose about what it's like to be at large in the wilderness—living, eating from the landscape, harvesting clams or catching fish or running around in your birthday suit, taking swims whenever you want. They were having the time of their life.

They took great photographs that have value for thinking about historical conditions. It's hard sometimes to figure out exactly where the Dimocks were, but even if you don't know exactly where they are, like this one shot they have, it's probably up in the headwaters of the Harney, and the thing is just full from bank to bank of lilies, probably bonnet lilies. When have you seen *that*? This may be indicative of the way fresh water flows were at the time and how they have changed. So the Dimocks give us some historical perspective of the mangroves of 1905–1906. Box camera, you know, climbing up on trees in the Harney to take pictures and lugging all this around.

People have asked me, because of my decade with big snakes, if there's a python book in me or some book about that experience. I have thought about writing a book in which you would learn stuff about pythons in the park, but it wouldn't be a chapter on how they reproduce and then a chapter on what they eat, and. . . . It would be kind of like Dr. Seuss in that book, *All the Places You'll Go*, about the places that pythons led me, the different roads I went down, by virtue of being inquisitive about them, a story of where they led me. You would come out of my book knowing something about those things, but that's not why you went into it. We'll see.

In general, I find the mangroves fascinating and attractive. I think it's because it's hard to experience them. They're not something you can walk up and look into like you can a canyon or look up at like a mountain. It's hard to grasp them. And if you do immerse yourself in them, it can be very different in its rewards on different occasions.

Some of the more memorable experiences I've had out there have been when it's been adverse, like one summer when we were out tracking manatees, lots of mosquitoes and lots of potential for thunderstorms. We got our job done, but it took longer than we had hoped, and there were literally thunderstorms all around us. We took refuge, parked ourselves on a chickee, which was immediately inundated by black clouds of mosquitoes. We just sat while it rained torrents and while the whole chickee just jumped out of the water from the thunder and lightning. We had our pants stuffed in our socks, our parkas closed so that we just had the little breathing hole because the mosquitoes were so dense. We did everything we could to not move much and give openings for mosquitoes, to just stay there and wait for things to pass. But I won't forget it. It was such a great feeling, one of those things where you feel like you've come out the other side of adversity, and you've triumphed. You feel good on the way back. So that was fun. I'll always remember that one.

Mangroves over the bow.
Photograph by Holly Genzen.

One day, I was at the Deering Estate, on their boardwalk that goes through the mangroves. It was a nice bright sunny day, a pretty strong easterly component to the wind, so water was being blown steadily on shore, and it was a rising tide. You could clearly see the water moving under the boardwalk, and the wind and then the sunlight all dappled and flashing. It was morning, mid-morning. We were looking east through all that filter and seeing all this light combined with the sound of water moving against the prop roots. There were leaves moving and all this dappling and the water lapping around. I closed my eyes and it almost sounded like it was raining, like a great steady summer rain. I don't know where else you would get that because of the way mangroves are structured and where they are, on that edge, interacting with other energies, the sun and the water, the tides and moon. It was pretty cool. I just fell in love with it.

Red mangrove prop roots with lichen (Pyrenula cirena). *Photograph by Anne McCrary Sullivan.*

PUTTING THAT PIECE IN THE JIGSAW PUZZLE

The Seaveys

LICHEN RESEARCHERS, EVERGLADES NATIONAL PARK

A bewildering variety of color and form are found in the lichens of Everglades National Park. Lichens can look like little shrubs, drape tree limbs like Spanish moss, or appear as little dots, lines, or smudges on the bark of trees. Their color range is wide. Red, yellow, green, gray, and white species are found in the area.

—Lichens in Everglades National Park, NPS brochure

We like to do things nobody has ever done before. The idea that maybe eight or ten billion have walked the world and we are the only ones that have ever done a certain thing intrigues us. And lichenology fell into that. Here in South Florida, a few people have made collections, but nobody has ever done a systematic inventory and then investigated, "How does the lichen relate to that tree or to that photo-habitat, or why is it in this habitat and not in a pineland?" Those sorts of questions intrigue us, and we're slowly, slowly beginning to unravel what is going on out there.

It's like you say to a person, "Well, you're the world's authority on myxomycetes." And he replies, "Yeah, the other guy died." That's basically where we are in lichenology in South Florida. Nobody else has ever done it, and it's just what we like to do in our retired life.

When we talk about lichens we're talking about the relationship between the fungi and the algae that make up a lichen. The fungi creates a safe habitat for the algae. It protects the algae from predators, from bacteria, and also from sudden changes in light. The algae can't take too much sunlight because ultraviolet light will kill it. But it has to have enough to do photosynthesis and make food to support both itself and the fungi. So, if a neighboring tree falls over and the lichen is suddenly in bright sunlight, the fungi has to make some quick adjustments. Fungi have learned to do this. Fungi can do a lot of things that we can't do. We can't, for example, metabolize our own antibiotics to protect us.

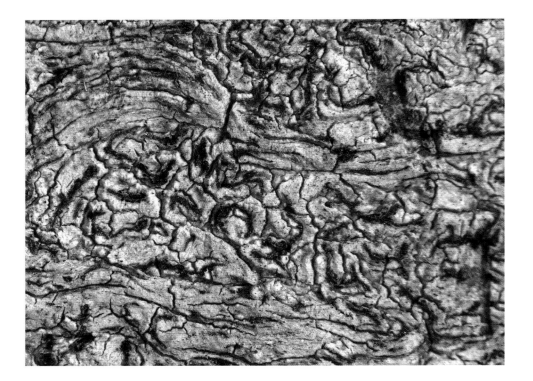

Enterographa murrayana. *The Seaveys described this lichen as new to science in 2014, publishing their discovery in* The Lichenologist. *This lichen has the ability to metabolize a chemical that filters ultraviolet light. Pharmacological research points to* E. murrayana *as a promising cosmetic ingredient to photo-protect human skin cells. Photograph by Jean Seavey.*

When you look out at the mangroves, you see all these prop roots and pneumatophores and you think of walking through those, how it almost takes ropes and pitons to get through. You think, wow, if there were vines up there, I could just swing across the top of the trees. Perfect Tarzan habitat. For fieldwork, we just climb on the roots and then swing across them from tree to tree, and if we see a lichen that doesn't look recognizable, we might collect it and take it back to the lab. When we collect, we always look around and make sure we're not collecting the only one. To us, that's very important. We've got to see at least four to six other individual pieces of that particular lichen out there before we will collect it.

Black mangrove has very rough bark, and it shades itself too much. Lichens don't like that. White mangrove is better. But of the three mangroves we have in South Florida, nothing compares with red mangrove for lichens.

You know, if you're walking the West Lake mangrove walkway there, you'll see orange blotches on red mangrove roots, the stilt roots (see photo on page 56). You can point that out from fifty feet away and say, "That's *Pyrenula cirena*." You know that's it because there's nothing else like it.

If you take a walk in almost any sunny place, you'll see blood red blotches on trees. That's *Pyrenula cruenta*. You can't mistake it for anything else, that's it. So you can learn those and wow your friends, not that they would really care probably. But some lichens you have to cut open and take a look at the interior in order to know what they are.

We canoe around the lakes, all those places ringed by mangroves, and we get off and walk into the forest. The ecotone just behind the mangrove forest—it can be a sawgrass prairie or the spartina prairies, juncus prairies, depending on where you are—the orchids just love that zone, and you'll have orchids growing on trees, sometimes in bloom.

Thursdays, Saturdays, and Sundays are our hiking days. I guess Sunday is the sacred day, the day the big hikes occur. And it's not just about lichens. Have you ever seen a mangrove fox squirrel? One of the most beautiful creatures in the world. They're quite shy. They'll climb up in a tree and get in a crack or crevice where it's very difficult to see the whole animal. But a dozen times we've got really good looks at them. They're gorgeous creatures, jet black with a white nose, white ear tufts, and white on the tail. It's striking.

One of our favorite places to hike is out Coot Bay Prairie to the south shore of Coot Bay and then just sit there and watch the birds fly around doing their thing all over the bay, just sit with a power bar, jug of water, whatever, and what more could you ask for? And when we have the time to sit and observe, we get to see things that other people don't see.

Rick: My brain always wants to know, "What is that scorpion doing climbing the tree? What is he after? Where is he headed? What is he going to do?" I might follow him for a while and try to answer some of those questions. Invariably, it winds up with some unanswerable question, and I call these "my mysteries." And then that's when I put on my Sherlock Holmes deerskin cap and I start to investigate, and I try to see if anybody has ever come up with the answer. A lot of people look at me and turn and start to back away when I talk about these things because they think I'm a little crazy, and I probably am, but this is my world, this is what I like to do.

Think about the many millions of birds that migrate through here, spring and fall. In the fall, as they head south, this is their last stopping-off spot. They have to feed, bulk up. And in the spring migration, as they're coming across the Gulf of Mexico or Caribbean, the first thing they see is the mangrove forest. They're tired and hungry and they've used up a lot of the fat they accumulated prior to their journey. They have to feed, bulk up again before they can go on to northern areas. This is the first place they stop.

So there's no better place to get a good look at warblers than the mangroves during migration. We have many thousands of square miles of mangrove forest, and if you go in times of migration, the warblers and cuckoos and all kinds of songbirds are just prolific.

Of course, where you have songbirds, you have their predators, owls and hawks, and you can see barred owls close up. Cooper's hawk, big, long tail, just sits there and waits and all of a sudden makes its move, and there goes a songbird. But that predator-prey relationship exists everywhere; we're all preyed upon by something. No matter what organism we are. It's just a factor of life. We feel fortunate to be able to view those sorts of things in action, and in mangrove forests you can view them pretty close up.

In the 1950s, '60s, water was shut off totally from Everglades National Park. With zero water entering the park from outside, there was a total change of vegetation. Aquatic plants died off. And we don't have any record of what was here before. So if we try to restore the Everglades, how do we know when we've got it right? We don't know what we're shooting for.

Well, Rick and Jean are doing an inventory of lichens. And one of the reasons for this is that, let's say a catastrophe hit and Everglades National Park was burned or plowed under, totally destroyed. Okay, now we're going to let it regrow. Because Rick and Jean have taken this lichen inventory, we've got a record of all the lichens. We don't know any other plants that grew here, but we know that lichens are a cryptogram, in that they produce spores in the air. They produce a number so high that we're breathing them as we sit here. They go up to the stratosphere, twenty kilometers up. They circle the Earth. They're so light, and they come down who knows how many years later. But they're there. The plants are gone, the trees are gone, but the lichens are there. If they drop to the ground, you'll have those lichens if they can find a suitable thing to grow on.

When we try to restore the Everglades after it's been totally demolished, how do we know we're getting it right? Well, we go to Rick and Jean's lichen inventory, and we see we do have some of these species, but we're missing another fifty species. Why? In the database, we find that a particular species only grows on a red mangrove in a certain light environment. Because we don't have that lichen, we know that we have to provide a space for red mangroves and the particular light zone they create. If we provide that, we've put that piece in the jigsaw puzzle. Now we go to another lichen, and we find that it needs a rough bark tree. Maybe it was only collected on mahogany, live oak, black mangrove. So now we know that we've got to fine-tune this system, take steps to provide for these rough-barked trees.

This is what we're trying to do. Not simply inventorying the lichens, but keeping a database on communities of lichens, the conditions in which they live. We hope to be able to use this information, in time, as a measure of plant community health. We ourselves are probably not going to live long enough to use it, but we're hoping that if we provide this data, somebody will see the worth of it. We'll pass it along.

East Cape in the aftermath of a storm. Photograph by Holly Genzen.

Mangroves sometimes anchor themselves in oyster beds and accumulations of shell. Photograph by Anne McCrary Sullivan.

We've found some species of lichens that are new to science, named them and published papers. One of these is *Enterographa murrayana*, which we named for the lady that colonized Murray Key (see photo on page 58). The story that's passed out is that Mr. and Mrs. Murray settled on Murray Key. He died at an early age, and she raised seven children on that key. I mean, stop and think about that. I don't know how old the children were when Mr. Murray died. I don't even know the gender of the seven children, whether they were all girls or all boys or whatever, but somebody had to go fish, take the dory out there and get supper. *Enterographa murrayana* honors Mrs. Murray, the Murray family.

Our love affair with the mangrove zone is an extension of being here a long time and having the freedom of not having a job, not having to work, not having to worry about money, just getting up in the morning and saying, "Well, what do we want to do today?" The answer is always some hike across part of the Everglades, and much of that exploration time has been in the mangrove zone, either canoeing around or walking through the mangroves, seeing the wonders, the orchids and things that are there. We like our solitary existence, and mangrove zones certainly provide that. The red mangrove roots are a wonderful area to stop and have lunch; you can always find a nice seat up in a tree, put your back against the trunk, sit on the prop root, have a place for both feet, be comfortable, and watch the world go by. Being out there is almost a spiritual experience, really, at least for us.

Jean: It's more than just studying. It's addictive once you get into it. It's a different world, something you've never seen, and it's different things to different people. Lots of things to some people, lots of different things to the same person.

Rick: The spiritual part is actually what we gravitate to. We seek that.

Jean: One of the first things we did when we visited down here was spend a week on a houseboat. And it was just exactly that, a spiritual thing. We went out to Tarpon Bay, anchored to the mangrove trees out there. We brought a canoe with us, and we took the canoe and paddled up the little creek, went back, back, back in the red mangrove forest. I don't know how far we went, most of the day, and finally the creek petered out, and we got out of the canoe and went *through* the mangroves about fifty feet, into a juncus prairie.

Rick: And we just kept going. Every once in a while we'd come to a buttonwood tree out in the middle of the prairie. I remember I climbed one. I wanted to be able to look out as far as I could see. I had the feeling when I climbed that tree, and this may be crazy, but maybe nobody had ever been there before.

The next day we just laid on the top of the houseboat. Every once in a while we'd look at the shore. Raccoons would come out and they'd be fishing for clams or whatever. There were wading birds along the edges of the shore, snowy egrets, great egrets, great blue herons. And ospreys, of course, taking their dives. It was fun to watch them circle, then hover, and all of a sudden . . . whoosh, smash into the water. Bald eagles that flew by and roseate spoonbills.

A lot of times you have a husband and wife where one is interested in something and the other one does it just to be with that person. Or maybe actually absorbs that love over time too, and so they share that. But Jean and I both love the same thing. We love being out in nature.

By the time we came to the Everglades, we knew most every plant in New England. Here, it was a new world, a new adventure, new plants, new flowers. And so people say, "What keeps you in Florida?" We say, "Well, we've got a big backyard that we haven't explored fully yet."

Sunset, Roberts River. Photograph by Holly Genzen

PART II
GOD
BLESS
CANOES

Storm front. Weather can change rapidly in inland rivers and bays as well as in the Gulf. As a weather system moves through, the sky sometimes indicates two different kinds of weather. Photograph by Anne McCrary Sullivan.

ATTITUDE IS THE DIFFERENCE BETWEEN AN ADVENTURE OR AN ORDEAL

Toby Nipper

CANOEIST AND WATER TRIBE RACER

D
ave and I never made a float plan, a destination, had any clues of tides, nor did we care. We both love wandering and have been misplaced on many of our trips. It gives me some extra training miles. I did not have charts and Dave's GPS is a touch screen that has been touched so many times it's unreadable. Trust me, this is fun not to know where you are and to figure it out. Hell, you are not gonna die, just be late.

One trip, we went to Panther Key. We had a breeze and right before dark, my favorite, no-see-ums. I skedaddled and went tent-bound at 17:30 and read. Awesome moon during the night. Only a few turtle nests and could not tell the ages as it had been raining.

Next morning, with the Canadian Bug Shirt's mesh full of the little flying teeth, the day came alive for us. We left our tents set up, set off to some other islands to see what the turtles have been up to, do some wayward exploring. Panther Key has a hard bottom so walking way out is easy. I love all the tracks made between the tides. Starfish are interesting to me, how they go in hippy patterns.

Back at camp the breeze was still nice, and the bugs were none, NONE! We sat quietly and looked. The big old moon started coming up and that area looked like it was on fire. The moon stayed red for a long while with a lot of lightning and cool air. Next morning, we took our time, waited way past good light, then left. We ran with an incoming tide, came out right at Totch Brown's island. Awesome. We were back at the trucks lickity spilt. Then my favorite—the Train Depot. All you can eat salad bar with peel-and-eat shrimp. The end of an awesome trip. All in all, you just got to get out there and play—and get lost.

I've been coming down here in this mangrove part of the Glades since the eighties, had me a custom-built flats boat. Then a buddy of mine talked me into buying a sit-on-top kayak. I'd paddle around to fish. Then I seen this little advertisement for Kruger canoes, built one at a time. I got to checking out Kruger canoes, and I ordered one. Never seen one. Never sat in one. The Kruger canoes led me to the WaterTribe. They were doing a race here in March that they do every year, first weekend in March, and I drove down to the checkpoint right in front of Kenny Brown's store and I couldn't believe it. They were paddling from Tampa to Key Largo, doing it in less than eight days. The longest trip I'd ever done was like eight miles in one day, which I thought was really fantastic.

I did my first WaterTribe Everglades Challenge, the "EC" it's called, running from Tampa to Key Largo, and when I got to Florida Bay I said, "I've found what I like doing."

I went home and asked my wife if she had anything she wanted to do. She wanted to go back to college and get her master's. I said, "Okay, but I'm going to quit my job." So I went in to Florida Power and Light, and I go, "I got eight weeks' vacation coming, I want all of them right now. I'll let you know what I'm doing after the eight weeks is up." And in eight weeks I went in and turned in all my cards and radios and keys and never went back to work.

My WaterTribe name is "Whitecaps." Every few years they do the "Ultimate Florida Challenge." That one goes all the way around the state. The first year the guy that won did it in nineteen days or something. Took me twenty-two days. See, it's like the EC. It's gonna be different every year. The weather has a total bearing on it so you can't know from one year to the next.

You get a shark's tooth for doing the EC. You get an extra shark tooth and also a gator tooth if you do the inside route since you had it a little bit harder. You do the all-the-way-around you get a shark's tooth for each day. You can get a gator tooth for one other part of it and you get a whale's tail for the last section. That's the big thing now. People come in with their necklaces and they'll see how gaudy they can be, like a bunch of kids in a gang.

Usually when we're doing a race, we try not to sleep over two hours at a time. I've gone fifteen hours without sleep and when you do that, you see stuff that's not really there. Your judgment gets bad. I've gotten to where I'll try to sleep at least an hour and a half somewhere any time of the day, just pull over and lay down inside and go to sleep for an hour and a half, two hours, and get up and go. If you're tired enough, you can sleep.

You have to do a check-in every twenty-four hours.

I don't eat as much as you would think. On the twenty-two-dayer all-around I think I used my stove only seven, eight times. I make stuff called "Logan bread." It was made by some explorer way back and there's all different variations of it. It's mostly whole wheat, got molasses in it, and it doesn't go bad, gets real hard. I eat a lot of that.

I done a very dumb thing, first EC, I think. I got to Bottle Key, only about seven miles from the finish. I'd been fightin' the wind, the waves, and was tired and it was getting late. I pulled in 'cause I knew if I got in around trees I could get out of the boat and stretch. Well, I got back in my boat, and the way the route should go was back out into the open water and then down towards Key Largo. I was like, "I'm tired. I don't want to do that. I want to cut across here." So I said, "I'll fly old 'Cracker Logic.' I'll go along and as long as I can see birds standing, I'll know it's shallow. Where I can't see birds, it's deep." So I'm going along, going along, going along, birds, birds . . . no birds. Then the boat stuck. Like I said, if you have sleep deprivation you end up being very stupid at times. Well, there's no birds. Of course not. It's almost dark. They all went to roost.

I took my shoes and PFD off and went over the side, but I couldn't stand up in the mud. I'd sink to my chest. So I laid on my side and wiggled like a snake, grabbed the line and pulled my boat to me, wiggled again, and pulled my boat to me. I tell you, I looked terrible when I come in.

I do not understand people that hire guides. Most of the fun for me is figuring it out, even if it's frustrating. Yeah, I been confused before and spent the night somewhere I did not plan on. Gone the wrong way? Yep. Been miserable with no place to camp? Yep. Been in a panic? Nope. Been scared? Yeah, a lot. Prayed once offshore.

You gotta have a mindset: I don't have nowheres to be, no time to get there. Instead of fighting it, just relax and go with it, work your way through and look. You see a lot of neat stuff sometimes.

Some people think it's terrible to come down here in the summertime with the bugs and stuff. We've got a five-part video on YouTube under "Pearlfella," doing the entire Wilderness Trail in August, Everglades City to Flamingo and the Nightmare.

As far as paddle boats go, I've got three. I don't own a kayak anymore. In kayaks, you never get a break and you're always wet, and everything you pack has got to be in multiple tiny bags. In a Kruger canoe, I can put everything in two big bags. It's got like twelve layers of Kevlar in key wear-points. They're almost indestructible. I've been out with twenty-two days' worth of supplies and never resupplied except for drinking water. I can sleep in it.

A good friend of mine, Everett Crozier, built me a boat they call a "Texas Water Safari Boat," nineteen feet long, carbon fiber. It's only thirty-something pounds.

On my long Hawaiian boat, I carry a Menehune. The way the legend goes, all Hawaiian boats have those little steps off the stern and that's so the Menehune, the little people, can get on and off the boat. Everett put a step on my boat for the

Menehune. I put on the WaterTribe message board, "I need a Menehune." Sandy Bottom, who has done a lot of races, was born in Hawaii. She had one at the start of a big race. I put it on the step on the back of the boat. Turned out a Menehune is a fertility goddess. Funny. Only two people on that boat weren't on Medicare.

If you go around the back side of Turkey Key, there's one tiny little beach and a bay in there where Charlie Creek comes out. You can cut through and go back to Darwin's if you want to. Well, during the winter months that bay goes almost dry on a full moon tide. We're in there one night and the tide's way out and we hear somebody walking in the water, *sploosh*, *sploosh*, *sploosh*. At first, we're going, "There's nobody out here." I got to thinking, somebody might have been way back up in there in that creek fishing, tide went out, and now they're trying to walk out or drag their boat out. So we shined the lights around, but nobody's out there. Later on, we heard what sounded like a horse or a cow in the water doing that "splooshing." We never could figure it out. This went on for a couple of years when we camped there.

When he was about four or five, I took my oldest grandson down here with my flats buddy. It was early in the morning, and I'd brought a spotting scope so he could look at stuff. I heard somebody wadin' out there again and I'm like, "What in the heck?" I got up and set up my scope and started lookin'—and what it was, the water gets real shallow, and a porpoise will run the mullet and get to going so fast that he'll beach himself in the mud. Then he has to take that fluke and flap, flap to turn hisself around. Well, being in that cove, it echoed. And that makes it sound like somebody's wading real fast in the water, and if there's two of them it sounds like a horse or a cow. It took me about four years to solve that little mystery. We started calling it "Turk, the Monster" ('cause we're on Turkey Key) just to scare people.

I got caught in a pretty bad storm one night about midnight. As it went by, I just sat back and said, "Okay. I'm not going to fight it. I want to sit here and relax, keep my boat turned into the waves, and make sure I'm not going to Mexico." I turned on my headlight and turned it back off 'cause it scared me looking at that water—it was up above me.

I got a thing on my boat that says, "Attitude is the Difference between an Adventure or an Ordeal." That's right on my boat, and it's true. You go with somebody that, the day's raining, and they're complaining, "It's miserable. It sucks." Well, they got a wrong attitude. Now they're going to make *me* miserable. It's like, "Oh, the bugs are awful. I can't stand it. I don't want to go anymore." It's fun to goof around about it, you know. Bill and I camp down here a lot, and we always go, "Well, will it be a one pillow trip or a two pillow trip?" You know, you got to have two so you can muffle the mosquitos whining at night. To complain would be like going on the Appalachian Trail and getting to Pennsylvania saying, "I hate rocks."

It's all attitude, mindset, and with some common sense, these trips work well. One of my mentors told me, "If you are cold, paddle harder. If you cannot sleep you need to be paddling." Wake up at 03:30 (like some of us old guys do), the hell with just laying there. Pack it up right then. Or if base camping, shove the boat off and do a loop. Skeeters are bad at camp, but once you get out there on the water, the stars are awesome! You just gotta know how to adapt.

The more of this I do, the more I find it is more about the people you do it with or what you get out of it than the toys. Toys are nice, though—a big tarp to sit under, a camp chair, some wine. Just be careful and know your toy will work for what you want. After all, a Kruger is just an overpriced canoe to some—overpriced canoe for the weekender, for sure! Come live in my world and see how nice it can be. Best advice I ever got from a beer-drinking buddy about buying or doing something: "You are dead a long time!"

Roots and wave at Florida Bay. Photograph by Anne McCrary Sullivan.

I love this one base camp, can stay there for days without ever leaving for a paddle. During the day I get to watch a lizard catch flies, see a red-bellied woodpecker hunt, listen to a lonesome heron just above you, watch big wasps in the morning digging holes. If the tides are right, I can do over a one-quarter mile hike out to the Gulf.

My Turk Monster came back the last night I was there, woke me up. This time it lasted a long, long while and got closer. Took me a long time to figure out the scary-man wading noises. Now, I just enjoy them. Spend some time in the summer down here and figure it out. Your own mind is the boogie man.

Roger Hammer with freshly caught snook. Photograph by Michelle Hammer.

MANGROVES, MANCHINEEL, AND GOD BLESS CANOES

Roger Hammer

NATURALIST, PADDLER, AUTHOR

When I went on my third solo Wilderness Waterway trip from Everglades City down to Flamingo, a buddy of mine, Keith Bradley, asked, "Are you going to paddle down the Rodgers River?" I said, well, I was going to stay at the Rodgers River Chickee, but I would probably go out the Broad River. He said, "Go down the Rodgers River." I said, "Why?" He said, "It's a pretty river, and you know. . . . Go down there." I said "Why?" He said, "Frank Craighead."

Craighead found a tree in the Everglades, a hibiscus relative called *Pavonia paludicola*. It has tiny green flowers, and it's rare as all hell. Keith said, "There's an herbarium specimen that Frank Craighead collected along the Rodgers River in 1962. Go look for it."

So, on my fourth day out, I'm paddling down the Rodgers River and discover that the tree is lining the banks of the river, and I have since found them along the Broad River too. I saw dozens and dozens and dozens of them, with orchids growing on their branches.

And I also looked for the old Rodgers plantation along the Rodgers River. I was looking for royal palms because the only record of wild ghost orchids in Everglades National Park was from Charles Torrey Simpson back in the early 1900s. He saw them growing on royal palm trunks at the Rodgers plantation. So, I paddle along looking for royal palms. Then I saw a couple of really big trees growing among the mangroves and, when I got over there and got out, they were two huge royal poincianas, a tree native to Madagascar, and I knew I was standing at the Rodgers plantation. I guess some hurricane, probably Donna in 1960, took the royal palms down. So, no luck finding ghost orchids.

Isn't it odd that people would choose to live out there? It's remote now, and back then it was as remote as any place could be in Florida. There was even a woman who lived on Murray Key south of Flamingo with her seven boys. God almighty, that's hard core. I'd like to have met her. Living out there on that island with seven youngsters. You know, they didn't have window screen then.

So anyway, when you're paddling down the Rodgers River, look for these small trees with little heart-shaped leaves and tiny green hibiscus-like flowers. They're an entirely different looking plant than anything else out there. And they're dotted all along that river on both sides.

Not long ago I was paddling up Buttonwood Canal and there was a guy fishing from a motorized canoe, and he was tied up to a poisonous manchineel tree. There's a bunch of them along that stretch of the canal, just before you reach Coot Bay. You can spot them easy because of their bright green shiny leaves with toothed margins. Of course, in winter they begin to lose their leaves, and that's when they're harder to identify. Eating the fruits can be fatal.

There's a movie, old, old, old movie, fifties. It's got Burl Ives in it, *Wind across the Everglades*. They've got this guy, they're dragging him off and you hear him screaming, "No! Not the deadly manchineel!" and then you hear him scream, "Aiiiiieeeeeeeeeeeeee!" I just crack up every time. I've seen half-naked kids in the Caribbean climbing the trees and jumping off into the water. So, if you don't get the sap on you, you're okay. Plus, the sap is water soluble, so if you're jumping in the water right after you touch it, it comes right off; it's not like poison ivy. Yeah, this guy, out of all those trees along Buttonwood Canal, he chose to tie his canoe to a manchineel.

One of my favorite places out there is the Shark River area. There are mangroves there today that are probably eighty feet tall. You look at their trunks and you go, "My God, what a glorious tree." Then you look next to it, and there's a trunk twice the size of that one that's been broken off by a hurricane long ago. If you look in the historical record, there were mangroves out there in excess of one hundred feet tall. Just in that area. You don't see mangroves that tall anywhere else that I've ever found out there.

Growing in the mangroves, there's a really pretty vine, the mangrove rubber vine with its stunning yellow-centered white flowers that look like morning glories. Its name is *Rhabdadenia biflora*, you know, *biflora* referring to two flowers because the flowers are almost always paired. And there's a wild allamanda with yellow flowers also growing up in the mangroves.

There are quite a number of orchids all along the Wilderness Waterway—the butterfly orchid, clamshell orchid, dollar orchid, mule ear, cowhorn. And the worm vine orchid, a vanilla with no leaves, just green or orange stems. Late May and June they bloom, and that is one spectacular flower—big, green, with this bright red trumpet-shaped lip sticking out.

One time in Hells Bay I was working my way through to get into Whitewater Bay, and I got all turned around, hit a dead end. I had to turn around and go back. I kept my wits about me and just went back to where I could see water flowing. The tide was going out, so I just followed it out.

On one of my Everglades Wilderness Waterway excursions, I was up in Huston Bay, and I angled a little bit wrong. So, I stopped and turned around and as much as I hated to paddle in the opposite direction, I paddled back until I could see a marker again. That's what I tell people to do. Don't keep going and try to figure it out. Go back until you know where you are and then go from there. This was before the days of GPS.

I've never really been lost out there, but the trail's been lost a few times. I've run into other people out there who were lost. One time I was coming down the Joe River in my powerboat and, as I passed one of the tributaries to the north, I saw a boat, and I thought I saw something red. I turned around and went back, and sure enough this lady was frantically waving a red jacket. She was hysterical, thinking she was going to die out there.

She was with her husband. They were trying to find their way out, and they ran out of gas. So, I towed them out into the Joe River and told them, "I'll go back and get a ranger and have them come and get you." But she was adamant that she was not going to stay out there because she was going to die. She hopped in my boat and left her husband there. And I'm thinking . . . I'm running off with the guy's wife and leaving him out there? I told him to get in my boat, and I took them both back.

Another time I was kayaking, and I came around Murray Key south of Flamingo in Florida Bay and the wind was howling out of the northeast, blowing hard, and I was on the south side of the key. I thought, when I come around that other side, I'm just going to bolt straight across to Bradley Key and then sneak along on the shore-line to get back. So, I came around the west side of Murray Key and saw what looked like a rental canoe on the south side of Oyster Key, a quarter mile to the west. I was getting ready to head to Bradley Key, and I looked over there and saw something red waving, like a distress signal. I looked again. It was definitely somebody waving some-thing red from that rental canoe. So, I thought I'd better go over there.

I had the wind at my back, so I was moving along pretty good, and as I approached, there's these two frantic college coeds. They're on spring break. They didn't have anything red to wave except the tops of their bathing suits, and I was like *Thank you, Lord, thank you, Jesus!* And they were so fearful they were shaking. They are right behind Oyster Key, and you can practically wave at people at the campground, but they couldn't paddle against that wind, and they just knew that if they got out there on the open water, they were going to get carried away and end up in the Gulf of Mexico. So, I tied a rope to my kayak and towed them back. It was a pretty hard paddle, and I finally had to say, "Don't paddle. Just let me pull you. That way it keeps the rope tight." If they paddle, it pulls up and then yanks back. It was like, "Put the paddle down, sit there and look cute, put your tops back on."

So, I run into things like that on occasion.

I've had some horrific experiences out there as far as weather conditions. One time I paddled back to Flamingo from Cape Sable at night because the wind was blowing so hard, I couldn't make it across that stretch of Florida Bay. I've had to do that three times now. Paddle at night to get away from hellish east winds. One of the hardest paddles I've ever had was coming down the Joe River into Whitewater Bay. It was January. That wind had to be blowing forty, forty-five miles an hour. It was horrendous. All of Coot Bay was breaking waves and foam piling up, big globs of it going airborne over the mangroves. What should have been a half-hour paddle across Coot Bay turned into a two-hour nightmare.

Recently, when I got my new Kevlar 16' 2" Swift Shearwater solo canoe, the first thing I did was load it up with gear and take it down to Flamingo. I paddled an eighty-five-mile loop, camping the first five nights at East Cape, Middle Cape, Northwest Cape, Shark Point, and Highland Beach, all beach sites. By the time I got to Highland Beach, I was tired of sand. Sand gets into everything so, when I left Highland Beach, I headed south to the Harney River, and there's shell mound that's been there since Hurricane Wilma in 2005, right square in the center of the north mouth. I pulled up onto the shell mound and removed everything from the canoe, washed everything off, took one of my waterproof duffel bags, put some biodegradable soap in it, put all my clothes in there and shook the hell out of it, washed everything and got rid of the sand. When I got to the chickee, I tied ropes to the supports and hung my clothes out to dry. I felt refreshed.

My next camp sites were Harney River, Shark River, Joe River, South Joe River, and they're all chickees, a bit of a blessing after all that sand and no shade. I landed back in Flamingo. Big loop. Very nice. Now I'm starting to stare at charts again.

View from the tent: mangroves behind Shark River Chickee. Photograph by Anne McCrary Sullivan.

Last May when I was out there paddling around, I discovered a population of butterfly orchids off the charts in color variation. This is a really common orchid, and normally the lip's white with a magenta blotch in the center. I found one out there where the entire lip was pink with a magenta center. And those lateral lobes that are snow white on every other one you ever see: pink. It was like "What the hell is that?" I'm paddling up there thinking I've found a new species or something.

Then I found one that instead of the sepals and petals being brownish green, they were creamy white, blushed with pink, and this big white lip with a magenta blotch on it. Then I found one that had almost solid bright green sepals and petals. It was like *holy cow*. These things are just bizarre.

It's what botanists would describe as a hybrid swarm. Perhaps some other gene pool is milling around among them, creating offspring that look totally different than what is normal. They've even suggested that the butterfly orchid itself might be a hybrid of two Bahamian orchids. The only place in the world where the butterfly orchid occurs is in Florida and three islands in the Bahamas. We write it off as such a common orchid in Florida, but it's rare when it comes to worldwide distribution.

One time when I was out fishing in my canoe, I was camping on the Harney River Chickee. At the center of the mouth of the Harney, there is a mudflat, and I watched five bottlenose dolphins came out of the Gulf as they swam right by me, and then all but one stationed themselves around this mudflat. They just floated there, not swimming, with their fins sticking out of the water. And then the fifth one bolted across that mudflat, mud flying, shells flying, fish freaking out, and the other dolphins grabbed the fish coming off the flat. *Holy moly.* That was, like, a planned attack. Big-time intelligence at work.

One other time I watched dolphins chase mullet up onto the beach at Cape Sable, and then they beached themselves and began grabbing the mullet flopping around on the sand. Just like killer whales do when they attack seals on beaches. So, stuff like that just keeps you going out there. And now sawfish seem to be making a comeback. I'm seeing them more often now than I did ten years ago. You can see them if you paddle around on the flats of Florida Bay, often just lying on the bottom.

I fish a lot when I'm out. I caught a really nice trout off of Middle Cape and then cooked it for dinner at Northwest Cape that evening. On that trip I brought three bottles of St. Peter's Cream Stout, my favorite beer in the world, and was planning to drink one at each cape to toast sundown, but I didn't drink one at East Cape because I arrived there so late. I got to Middle Cape and ended up enjoying one with the sunset there. Then I got to Northwest Cape and I realized that the ice wasn't going to last any longer. I was forced to drink the remaining two as the sun set over the Gulf. So, it turned out to be a nice happy night.

I would say on a seven-day trip I probably eat fresh fish three or four times. I don't know what possesses people to do this, but so many people run out and buy canned Vienna sausages and Beanie Weenies to take out camping. Other than gallon jugs of water, I usually don't pack any cans or bottles. I buy fresh vegetables, remove them from their containers and put them in Ziploc bags. I bring fresh corn, potatoes, asparagus spears, Brussels sprouts, and carrots, then just trim everything up, and wash everything beforehand. I'll never forget one time I was at the Rodgers River Chickee and I'd caught a big, fat redfish and had already filleted it and chopped it up into boneless chunks. And these two French Canadians in sit-inside kayaks arrive, and the Rodgers River Chickee was their first night from Chokoloskee. They must have launched early because it's about thirty miles from Chokloskee to the Rodgers River Chickee.

So, they're on the other side of the chickee with a little folding stove and cooking freeze-dried God-knows-what. And on my side, I'd taken the chunks of redfish, rolled them in cornmeal, and fried them to a golden brown. I had steamed asparagus spears, a steamed ear of corn, and some Merlot in milk-carton-type containers. So, I had Merlot and fresh corn and asparagus spears with a little bit of butter and a squeeze of lime and fresh fried fish. And these guys are over there like Cro-Magnon Man. And I thought, "God bless canoes."

I looked at their itinerary and their next night was to be spent at the Shark River Chickee, and the night after that was Flamingo. Why such a hurry? I haven't a clue. I thought, "You guys are missing the point here."

May is my favorite month to paddle in the Everglades. April is usually windy. It starts calming down at the end of April, and then May is typically picture-perfect for paddling. It's not blazing hot yet, you don't have to worry about a cold front coming through, and the mosquitoes are at tolerable levels. The wormvine orchids are in flower, maybe some of the butterfly orchids too. The tourists have long ago gone. That's my favorite month to be out there, May.

And I like going solo, especially for the decision-making, like, "Where do I go tomorrow, and which way do I go?" No collaboration necessary.

I was talking to my friend Tony Terry. He's a law enforcement officer in Everglades National Park down at Flamingo, real nice guy. The first time Tony and I ever met, I was camping on Middle Cape, and you know that plant, *Scaevola*? It's a nonnative invasive plant called beach naupaka. There was a bunch of them growing on Middle Cape, and I thought, I'll just do my civic duty and help get rid of them. I had a powerboat that time, so I backed it up near shore, took the anchor rope and tied it to the stern and then I'd run up there on the beach and tie the other end to a *Scaevola*, and then I'd just get up on a plane and all of a sudden, this plant would go flying out of the ground into the Gulf. So, while I was doing that, Tony was coming around the Cape. He looks over there and sees this boat hauling ass when this plant comes flying off the beach into the water. He's like, "What in the hell is that?" He still talks about it. He says, "I get out there and there's this wacko guy, some old hippie, yanking plants off the beach."

Not long ago, I spent a couple of hours flying over the mangroves. The inspiration was that I needed photos for the new edition of my book, *Exploring Everglades National Park*. And there's this woman pilot, Yogini Modi, who owns Orient Flight School and flies a Cessna out of Homestead General Airport, and I hired her. It was in the height of tourist season, and one of the things I wanted to do was photograph people camping on Cape Sable. We got to Cape Sable, and there wasn't one solitary soul. I wanted to put a parachute on and jump out of the plane. There was absolutely nobody.

But I got good pictures of East Cape and the Roberts River Chickee. And the Hells Bay region where the aerial view makes you say, "That looks like hell." It's pretty daunting to look down from the air and see where you've been paddling all these years, the maze of islands and creeks and tributaries that look like an incomplete puzzle.

Royal tern at Wilderness Waterway marker 93. Photograph by Anne McCrary Sullivan.

One of the classes I teach is for the volunteers at Fairchild Tropical Botanic Garden on the human and natural history of South Florida. I ask, "How many people here have been to Everglades National Park?" And every single time, only about half of them raise their hand. So, I talk about some of my adventures out there, and the first question out of their mouth is, "Aren't you scared?" And I'm going, you know, it's scarier driving in Miami. I'm sure you've heard of people getting killed in car wrecks, but how many people have you heard of getting killed canoeing in the Everglades? So, I don't know. People just don't understand.

A brown pelican (Pelecanus occidentalis) perches in a buttonwood tree. Photograph by Holly Genzen.

You know, every time you go out you see something different. The last time I paddled out there, I was leaving Highland Beach across that big expanse of the Broad River, and I paddled upon the mother of all tiger sharks cruising there. I paddled right up next it and I could see a cadre of remoras attached to its sides. It was probably around fourteen feet long. A good reminder of why you shouldn't go swimming in that area.

You can go out there as many times as you want in a year, and every single time you go you'll see something that you haven't seen before. I've had crocodiles crawl up out of the Gulf onto the beach at East Cape and dig nests while I'm sleeping at night. You'll hear them digging, thinking they're sea turtles, and then you get up and go, wait a minute, that's not a sea turtle.

I keep going back. Part of it is wilderness. There's not that much left in South Florida, especially in Miami. And that's another thing that I try to point out to people who live in Miami. Here you have this megacity with two million people, and you can be out sitting on the pristine beach of Cape Sable, and oftentimes be the only person out there. Twelve miles of glorious beach all to myself, and then at night you can look to the east and see the glow of lights from Miami. That's certainly part of it for me, the solitude. A lot of people don't like solitude, which makes it good for those of us who do.

BAM! A NICE HIT FROM A PRETTY LARGE SNOOK

Vivian Oliva

CANOEIST AND ANGLER

Blog: Today would be my fishing day. It was a beautiful windless day with perfect paddling conditions. The plan on these trips is basically to troll and stop here and there where there might be an opportunity to cast to a few points or see an interesting shoreline. But you don't stop moving to really work an area. The tide was perfect, a morning incoming, which is the best tide to fish these islands as you can get near them with the higher water levels.

Since the 2005 hurricanes, a lot of dead tree branches and trunks are scattered about the water. When the water is low enough they provide cormorants a place to hang out while drying their feathers. They have also created some new fishing areas. As I round the point at Mormon Key I start catching small trout and then much larger trout. I must have hooked and landed over 50 fish before I got to Turkey Key. It was a mixed bag of trout, jacks, and, of course, ladyfish. Not glamorous but a great time for someone that hasn't been fishing in almost a month.

I was born in Cuba. My family came here in 1962—I was three years old at the time—so I'm basically a Floridian, been here all my life. Fishing has always been a family thing. My mom and I used to pester my poor father to take us out. He wasn't a fisherman; he worked the graveyard shift, but every morning in the summer he'd come home and take me out to Biscayne Bay to fish off the bridges. I would wait for him with my fishing rod and tackle box ready.

I started out bridge fishing and I always thought, "I'd like to just get a little bit further out. I'd catch more fish." I bought a small fifteen foot aluminum skiff, started going to Biscayne Bay and the Keys. I didn't know about the Everglades. I didn't know Flamingo existed.

Sean McMullen, an avid fisherman and captain back in the eighties, said, "Why don't you go to Flamingo?" I said, "Where's that?" He gave me a map and off I went into the National Park. I thought, "This is beautiful!"

When I went out in my skiff and saw Whitewater Bay, I couldn't believe my eyes. It's like an inland sea. I started looking at the chart of the area, and I thought, "Oh my God, it would take me years to

figure this out. There are so many rivers, creeks, bays, and then there is Hells Bay."
The possibilities got me dreaming of future adventures. Every weekend I plotted out
a section of that vast area and over time, meticulously made my way to every spot I
could get into with my boat. Eventually, I started getting too far out and would have
to bring my camping gear to spend the night.

One day I was heading out the Buttonwood Canal to camp at Graveyard Creek,
and these kayakers were heading out. They were all in white. The boats were white,
they were dressed in white—a vision, perhaps. I was looking at them and said, "Where
are you guys going?" They said, "We're going to Chokoloskee. We're going to do
the Wilderness Waterway." I was shocked because my boat was full of garbage bags. I
packed everything in ugly bags. I said to myself, "How did they get all that gear into
those little boats?"

I became very curious about kayaks. Then I won a trip to Cabo San Lucas back in
about 1990, and that's when I found out they had sit-on-top kayaks you could fish
from. I was hooked! As soon as I got back to Miami, I bought a yellow Scupper Pro
sit-on-top kayak, twin hatch without rudder.

Then I had to learn how to camp from a kayak. And I didn't understand tides,
how they related to paddling. I started going out at night to Picnic Key on the Gulf,
an arduous six-mile journey *against* the tide. Imagine moving through wet cement—
that should give you some idea of the intensity of this tidal area. I didn't know any
better. I didn't realize you can work the tides in your favor. After that horrid adventure I installed a rudder on the boat and made myself learn tide prediction as it
applied to kayaking from point A to B.

For about four years my Scupper Pro was adequate for short trips, three-day
adventures, but it was killing me on longer trips. These plastic kayaks are slow, very
wide and heavy, and they require a lot of energy to push through water when they're
loaded with gear. So I got a long, sleek, sit-inside touring kayak, and that was awesome. But, in the backcountry that I love, it's very hard to get out of a touring kayak
to do anything, like to pee. It's also hard to get into and out of muddy sites. And
chickee camping, getting get yourself and your gear in and out of the boat, becomes
an event we call "chickee gymnastics," not yet an Olympic sport but definitely an
exhibition.

Then one day, a bunch of guys came into Watson's Place with solo canoes. I
thought, "Wow, these solo canoes are simple, beautiful, and light." I bought one.
But I was scared because I didn't know how to paddle it compared to a kayak, and
I always thought that a kayak would be more seaworthy than a canoe. I didn't think
you could go out in the ocean or into big water in a canoe. But that was just my fear.

Roseate spoonbills with pelican.
Photograph by Constance Mier.

My Hemlock Kestrel solo canoe is nine years old, and from what I can tell, should give me at least another ten years or more of good fishing. I like being able to change positions from sitting to kneeling on long trips, and I like being dry and warm. I have a carbon, bent shaft canoe paddle, made for racing. It only weighs ten ounces. Ten ounces. Can you imagine? It's like a box of Kleenex.

Blog: Darwin's Place is one of my favorite places in the Everglades. It is full of snook and beautiful birds. There have been times when the alligator population is large, but I have not had problems fishing around them. Today would be a different story.

At camp I switched to my St. Croix travel rod that I keep in a rod case for days off from paddling. I attached a 3000 Spheros reel and tied on a gold shad tail with an 1/8 oz. red cottee jig head. I set up my cooler near my seat back, pliers, tackle dry bag, lip gaff, and was on my way.

Clearing the first creek I came across my usual snook spot and cast. Bam! A nice hit from a pretty large snook that came up shaking his head from side to side. It headed towards one of the many deadfalls in the creek and I was afraid I couldn't stop it. Meanwhile, from the corner of my eye, I spotted a very large alligator right next to my canoe, very interested in the hooked snook.

Now, I am not usually scared of alligators but this one was intent on my fish and the creek was not big enough for all of us to respect our distances. At this point I had lost control of the snook and let it wrap up and break off in the snag. I moved on to the next bend.

The second bend in the creek was a spot where I had had some action in the past. Stopping to tie on a new lure, I discover that I brought my clothes bag instead of my fishing bag. Ugh! Luckily, I keep a small tackle box behind my seat. I tied on a space guppy shad tail and started casting, working the deadfall and snags around the bend. I get another hit and see that numerous gator heads are now coming up to the surface. Never have I been surrounded by so many alligators in here.

At this point I am hesitant to fish in this creek. Too bad, because there are fish here. But I continue to the large lake and the winds start up with sporadic rain. Working the shorelines I get no takers. Those dang fish are all in that alligator infested creek. What to do? I muster enough courage to go back to the fish and try to ignore the alligators, but with every cast, they are getting more interested. I decide to give up fishing and just enjoy the creek for the beautiful place that it is. The alligators win.

Very few women fish in the Everglades like me. I'm the only woman that I know that fishes out of a solo canoe. I'm often camping with a lot of guys. But I don't like having salt water on my skin. It makes me itchy. So I'll rig a tarp between trees or in a chickee so I can take a shower. If not, I'll take a body bath in my tent. I cut a three-by-three plastic sheet from a drop cloth and lay it on the tent floor, use my cook pot and pour in one cup of water and a capful of No Rinse Body Bath, use a bandanna to wash off and towel dry. Feels wonderful after a hot day before changing into "evening wear."

One of the things I love to do is go off-trail, find unmarked ways to get from point A to point B, away from motor noises and general paddler traffic, just for the quiet. And for the satisfaction of completing a run without getting lost. Marked routes are historical routes that were taken by bootleggers and gator hunters and such, but you can spend your lifetime zigzagging through these areas. There are so many possible routes. The website, Everglades Exploration Network, explains ways to get through, away from the Wilderness Waterway, the "magenta line."

I do a lot of planning, print out satellite imagery. The planning is part of the fun. And if it's a very complicated route like Hells Bay, then I'll print a notebook of the different maps, so I can flip through them and see where I am in case my GPS fails.

You know, I love Lopez and Rabbit Key even though they're so near. There's something special about those places. There's something magical about watching that river flowing by at the Lopez camp-site. When daylight's ending and that glow fills the sky it's so beautiful, and then the quiet is interrupted by dolphins cruising by.

Blog: It was 5:30 a.m. when we shoved off towards Lopez. In the darkness and quiet we paddled past the Chatham River in relative calm water and made a decision to take the quickest path towards Sunday Bay before the sun came up. We took a break at 9:00 am when the winds started gathering speed. As we paddled to the protected NE shoreline of Sunday Bay, I decided to start working a few of the coves in Sunday Bay. It was great! Lots of trout, feisty jacks, plus one big 'ole redfish which is now my last big fish of the year. After that we took the last of the outflowing tide to Lopez. We set up camp and had a relaxing afternoon with wine, dinner, and dessert. Another beautiful paddle and gorgeous sunset at Lopez.

Approaching the Gulf. Photograph by Constance Mier.

The silence. The silence. To be away from the noise and be in the wilderness. Traveling with the rhythm of the Everglades by working the tides, traveling slow enough to really experience the subtle beauty of this wilderness has become a passion for me. With the powerboat I sped along covering miles but never really seeing or hearing anything. I want to slow life down, really enjoy it. I also want to get there under my own power. As I get older, this is becoming more important to me. I am still learning, experimenting with new routes, new techniques, and different paddle craft, great ways to fully enjoy this gift we share in Florida, the magnificent Everglades. I feel like the Everglades are my home.

Night sky over young mangroves. Photograph by Contance Mier.

THE CANOE CAME FIRST AND THE CAMERA FOLLOWED

Constance Mier

PROFESSOR AND PHOTOGRAPHER

June 2009, I get a call from one of the guys that helps the park clear out the Bear Lake Canoe Trail. He says, "You got to go with me to Mud Lake because I just saw thirty flamingos back in there." He said, "I saw all this orange and I thought it was a bunch of kayaks. I got close and there were thirty flamingos just hanging out. You've got to go in there and photograph them." So I met him at the marina at 5:30 in the morning and we drove down that pothole infested dirt road to the launch site on the Buttonwood Canal.

The air was completely black with mosquitoes. Before getting out of my air-conditioned sanctuary, I put a frozen Camelback bladder into a small backpack and put that on, then put my bug jacket on over my long-sleeved cotton shirt and my wide-brimmed hat. I wore heavy canvas pants. I Velcroed my pant leg openings around my wool socks, put on sneakers and thick cotton gloves. Completely sealed and protected, I stepped out of my car into the loudest, most incessant, high-pitched sound I have ever heard. It was a mosquito festival, and I was crashing their party. Once I got over that shock and realized that they could not penetrate my barrier, I went about my business of getting the boat with the camera gear into the water.

We headed out the Buttonwood Canal and through Coot Bay and the creek into Mud Lake. Mud Lake's huge. Bob says, "Okay, well, that's where I saw them the other day. The birds were not there. The space was empty of pink color. I'm looking and thinking, "There's terrible light over there."

We keep paddling. I'm thinking, "God, this lake is huge. We're never going to see these flamingos. They're gone." I paddle and paddle and we go around a point and I look to the right, and just when my heart begins to sink, I spot a large pinkish aberration several hundred yards away, standing out against the greens and browns of the mangrove shoreline. There were sixteen or seventeen of them, and they were in perfect light. I paddled to within one hundred feet, staked out my boat, and sat for three hours photographing flamingos (photo on page 90).

It was mesmerizing to watch them feeding in the grass and mud. The sun blazed hot, but I never felt an ounce of discomfort. I had never seen flamingos in the wild and never realized how large they are. The largest of the group stood over five feet tall. They were busy feeding. I watched one bird move its legs back and forth quickly in the water, similar to what a snowy egret might do when foraging. It appeared that at any given time, half of the group would have heads submerged while the other half would be looking about. Once, something got the group's attention, and they simultaneously stood upright and faced the same direction.

There were two deep orange flamingos that were larger than the rest of the group. They seemed to invite interactions with the others on occasion. The interaction would usually begin with a bird coming up to the larger bird with what looked like a kiss. Upon closer inspection of the photographs, they appear to be biting, not kissing.

The Pauline Reeves Gallery in the Everglades Museum had my exhibit in November. One of my flamingo shots was there, and people at the reception would look at the photograph and go, "Where did you photograph those, in Miami?" Everybody thinks they're at the zoo. So I tell them I had to paddle five miles on a June morning to get to them.

Flamingos. Because it was assumed that Florida's native flamingo (Phoenicopterus ruber) had been hunted out of existence by the plume trade, local sightings were thought to be escapees from zoos or from the Hialeah racetrack flock. After careful research, however, it has been determined that South Florida continues to have a native wild population. Sightings are rare and have occurred at Mud Lake, in Florida Bay, and in the Keys. Photograph by Constance Mier.

The driving force behind all this is being on the water. I let the water and my canoe guide me toward photo opportunities, not the other way around. I think it was Dorothea Lange that said that the camera's just a camera. It's just there to help you see what's out there. And even though I might count on one hand the number of birds I saw at eye level on a particular day, it is worth every second of being on the water.

Photography opportunities in the Everglades are influenced by many things—the weather, tide, schedule, time of day, direction of the sun, time of year, marine conditions, etc. If all I did was go out there and spend all my time at one location, I believe the variety of images captured over time would be outstanding because any one or all of those factors will differ on any given day. For that reason I keep going back to familiar places.

Recently, I went out by myself for the first time ever. I went to Tiger Key a couple days. The plan was to go out and photograph. It's all I wanted to do. I didn't want to be responsible for anybody else's welfare, I just wanted to go out there and photograph. There's a beautiful mangrove I was just dying to get at the right moment with all the clouds and everything. I spent two days hanging out on that island. With the bugs. And the heat. I wanted to do it at a time of year when there's nobody out there. I was curious to know how I would feel out there alone.

It was amazing. I felt totally at home. At no time did I experience fear, only peace. I have since been out there again alone. Each trip was fantastic, and neither was exceptionally challenging although the heavy fog on one trip was intense. I was alone on Tiger when the fog rolled in. Never saw the sun again from about 1:00 p.m. until the next morning. It was both eerie and beautiful. And I had a blast with my camera.

Whenever I need a quick Everglades fix, Chokoloskee Bay is where I go. It is not an easy place to photograph. In fact, it is downright harsh. The bay is riddled with oyster bars. Of course, oyster bars are where the birds are found, and if I wanted to photograph them, I had to learn how to ease my way toward them while making sure my boat did not get sliced to pieces by unrelenting oyster shells. With so much shell, staking out is also challenging. I often resort to sticking one foot out of the boat and into the shallow waters. But it can be rewarding, as birds take advantage of the exposed oyster beds, a buffet table of marine edibles.

Every time I launch from Chokoloskee, I look toward the southwest end of the bay where the Chokoloskee and Rabbit Key Passes begin their run out to the Gulf. Near those channels are oyster bars where, during the winter months, white pelicans hang out. In summer, the bars are feeding and resting grounds for roseate spoonbills. Depending on the time of year, when I gaze across the bay, I see either a wall of white or a wall of red.

Come September and October, the terns return in force, and I have fun with them near the marina where they roost with brown pelicans on pilings. I anchor and sit with dozens of birds surrounding me. Ibises are common, and yellow-crowned night herons and oystercatchers.

The oyster flats of the bay look like out-of-control mud, but there is something beautiful about all of it, with the prop roots of the mangroves and reflections of green leaves. Mangroves and oysters go together well out there.

Mangroves are lovely, but when it comes to photographing, I find them the most difficult subject. They are shadowy, muddy, oyster-encrusted, messy, and unkempt in their green and brown presentations. Not very photogenic at first glance. But oh, those prop roots are intriguing, and when the light hits them just so, they do become photogenic with their sensuous shapes. I explore their mysteries through the lens. They are trees of the sea and I love them.

To get into Charley Creek from Turkey Key, tides have to be just right. You can't just go in there any time you want. The first time I went in that way, we left Turkey Key early and got into Charley Creek, entered the dark mangrove tunnel just as the sun was beginning to rise. By the time we got out the sun had come up and this world just opened in front of us—a line of mangroves, and just on the other side, a prairie, and there are hundreds and hundreds of birds including white pelicans (see photo on page 94). Between me and them were thick mangroves and mud. I found an opening, pulled my boat up the mud bank and staked out. I stepped onto a dead branch that was large enough to support my foot and proceeded to get out, one hand on a tree branch, the other holding my camera with 400 mm lens. As soon as I got my other foot out of the boat, I sank above my knees in mud. With two steps forward I was on firmer, grassy ground and very quietly went past the mangroves, heading toward the bird scene.

White pelicans (Pelecanus erythrorhynchos) are seasonal in south Florida. At the end of the winter season, they gather in large numbers before migration. Photograph by Contance Mier.

I've never seen so many birds in one place in my life. The water holes they were congregating around must have been loaded with marine edibles. I felt like a kid in a candy store. The challenge was that this is a totally wild place and birds have lots of choices, one of which is to stay far away from an intruder. They react right away to my presence, and birds are flying and moving around.

I started capturing as much as I could, but I was on a trip with four other people, and I couldn't stay. And this was not an area to get stuck in at low tide. I got my muddy self back into the boat and we continued exploring, but I vowed that I would go back there, set up a little blind before it got light, sit, and wait for them, wait for the sun to come up.

In January one year we noticed white pelicans flying overhead, coming and coming, hundreds and hundreds of them. At Pearl Bay that night we set up camp, and this gentleman and his son were camped on the other chickee. Turns out he used to be a fisher guide there and he gave us this amazing tip. He said, "You got to go back, there's a little creek and you can't really see it on the map but get back in there and there's a bay. That's where all the fish are."

The next morning before the sun came up, we worked our way back into this hidden bay, and I sat there and thought, "Those pelicans are going to come back." Sure enough, they did.

The white pelicans that morning were so close to my boat that I could almost reach up and grab them. Their wings beating were loud, like big fans, like "*Woosh, Woosh, Woosh.*" And hundreds and hundreds of them flew overhead.

Ask me if I got a photograph of them. I didn't. It was too dark. But stuff like that just blows me away. And you don't see that from the Flamingo marina. You have to paddle out there to see it.

It was nearly a full moon one weekend, and the tides were strongly affected, which meant that bait fish were being swept out of the backwaters. This meant that large predatory fishes such as sharks would be in the shallows. This also meant that the birds would have lots to eat. The area of the rookery was full of activity. The water was boiling, mullet jumping everywhere, schools of tiny bait fish sprinkling the water's surface. The sharks were there, coming right along the edge of the mangrove islands. One came up on my boat from behind and then made a violent wake in an attempt to get away.

From a distance I could see mangrove canopies saturated with white birds. Brown pelicans in great number intermingled with the great white egrets. It was hot, the sun never covered with clouds. This is the time of year I crave. The heat can zap your

Diving pelicans. Plunge diving is a signature behavior of brown pelicans (Pelecanus occidentalis). Able to dive from as high as 65 feet, they can hold up to 3 gallons of water in their throat pouches, then drain the water before swallowing their prey. Since the Environmental Protection Agency banned DDT in 1972, the brown pelican population, once decimated, has rebounded. In Florida, they breed primarily on mangrove islands. Photograph by Constance Mier.

energy quickly, but I am acclimated and was thrilled to sit among hundreds of birds all morning, knowing that I would not leave this place until the next day. Two glorious mornings among the smells and sounds of the birds—watching, studying, listening, learning. I am mesmerized by their lives, how they instinctively survive one day to the next.

I recorded the rookery sounds with my voice recorder. I can now distinguish the noises a bit more. The baby pelicans sound like mooing cows. The snowys sound like gurgles or like someone trying to talk underwater. Baby egrets make a constant chirp, and when the adult comes with food, the sounds rise to loud crescendos. Pelicans do the same. It's an amazing sound, could probably drive some people crazy, but to me, the sounds are entertaining.

The babies have raging appetites. The young egret is voracious, and I notice that it obtains food when mom sticks her head inside its mouth. Many times, there's a struggle as the baby clamps its sharp, powerful beak around mom's beak, and there's a tug of war.

Sometimes I look at my photos as archival data or amateur field research. In 2009, I visited a rookery in Everglades National Park three times: February 22, March 31, and May 17. In that sequence of photos,

North River Chickee.
Photograph by Holly Genzen.

I can follow the growth of young birds. I look at the photos and know that in February, both great white egrets and brown pelicans were mating and preparing nests in great numbers. In March, they were raising their babies, and in March some brown pelican babies were almost as large as the adults. In May, some young pelicans were already flying. The great white egrets did not appear to be fledging, but there were several groups of young ones established throughout the canopies of the rookery island.

By contrast, in 2010 we had barely recovered from one of the longest sustained cold snaps experienced in South Florida. I believe it was this rare event that delayed the nesting of the birds. Again, I made three visits: February 20, March 21, and April 25, and I witnessed a very different timeline of nesting.

In February 2010, brown pelicans were in large number and busily nesting, but there were only a handful of great white egrets and even fewer pairs settling in with a nest. In March, the brown pelicans looked much the same as in February, and the great white egrets had finally grown in number. Still, compared to 2009, there were far fewer.

I finally did see the rookery teaming with both browns and great whites, and even a few snowy egrets. But I only saw one baby pelican. It was very small compared to the larger version witnessed a year before. There were some baby egrets, but still too small to be sticking their long necks out. I did get a photo of the baby pelican feeding from its mother's very large pouch.

In the meantime, some of the adults were busy flying in and out, still trying to score a stick here and there. Lots of squabbling among the adults, mostly within species, but sometimes I would see a pelican and egret go head-to-head. It appears that the egrets are much more aggressive and probably more dangerous with their sharp beaks. I noticed a dead adult pelican hanging from the trees. It had been there for some time; all that was left were the feathers and a few bones. There it hung. I imagined an egret causing great injury to the bird. What else could it be? Old age? Sickness? Generally, the birds seem to have survived this cold winter. The Everglades lives on, passing from one generation to the next. And among the thriving nests comes death for one of the adults.

I think one can go through life believing they are in control. But step outside of that ordinary reality and explore the wilderness, and it becomes apparent that absolutely nothing is in your control. I believe this is why so many people do not enjoy being

Hells Bay sunrise.
Photograph by Holly Genzen.

in wilderness. Out there the weather, the tides, the water, the animals we try to pho-tograph—none of those things do we have control over. Out there you are only an observer. Once you accept that fact, many gifts start coming your way. These gifts are often not easy to come by; they require experience, perseverance and patience, innovation and problem solving, and sometimes just plain luck. As you accept chal-lenges, allow yourself to let some things go, you become a better paddler, a better navigator, a better photographer. You realize that you can photograph these beauti-ful Everglades, but only on their terms.

Sea Grape. Photograph by Holly Genzen.

CAROUSING WITH THE HAPPY HOOFERS

Bill Leonard

CANOEIST AND HAPPY HOOFER

When Virginia and I came to South Florida, we opened the newspaper and read that the Florida Trails chapter, the Happy Hoofers, were having a meeting in downtown Ft. Lauderdale. We said, "Let's go!" Ken Carpenter was the person that ran Wilderness Waterway trips for the chapter, as well as shorter trips. He made us feel right at home. That very weekend we were on a canoe trip in the Everglades.

Our first long trip was to Cape Sable. We went out in a big old seventeen-foot Old Town Tripper with whitewater paddles. I remember, we were on the beach and at about six o'clock everything became still, the sea was like glass, and a swarm of bugs moved out from in back of us. I'm cooking, and my hand is covered with no-see-ums and mosquitoes. So we jump in the canoe and paddle offshore to flee them.

Bugs. Yeah. The big attacks are right at dusk. Fortunately, I already had the tent up. When we finally crawled into the tent, we brought a host of bugs in with us. It was a tough night, and it was a hard paddle back the next day because the water was rough.

Everglades paddling is a wholly different type of paddling, and over the years of tides and winds, I've been where I expected to pass right through an area, but wind had blown the water out of the bay. Doesn't take much wind to blow the water out of one of these shallow bays, and then high tide is still low tide especially when the fronts come through. I never did get stuck, but we almost got caught in the Nightmare once. It's a tidal creek that goes out both ways, but there's a side creek that dumps out into the Gulf, and we jumped out there, then followed the Gulf and headed up the Harney River.

With a former member who's passed away, Lou Adams, we planned a trip out of Everglades City and down the Gulf. First night, Pavilion Key. It was a little rough getting there. The raccoons there are out in the daytime, and one of our members lost his bread immediately. We had a big group. Ken is expert in inviting people that I think shouldn't be out there, not experienced, not qualified. There was one couple I'd never met.

The next day, I bet the winds were gusting to better than thirty knots, and we had a long paddle ahead. This couple had an old canoe with the single thwart in the middle. That canoe was actually flexing, I could see it, and they were shipping some water. We made it to Mormon Key and got set up and I told Ken, "We've got to send these people back." The woman was totally exhausted.

He said, "Oh, no, they can make it."

I said, "They can't. She's exhausted."

They went to set up their tent, and out came a tent with plastic poles. A pole breaks. I had some aluminum tubing to repair that, but some fishermen showed up, and I said, "They can't do it." So the fishermen said they would go to the Ivey House and get Dave to come out and pick them up. Dave showed up while we were taking off the next day.

When you run the Wilderness Waterway, you've got to stay on schedule because your campsites are reserved. So now we're a day behind, maybe half a day, but the outside seas calmed down, so we made it up. We got down to Highland Beach and the next day we went swimming in Graveyard Creek, had a good night, and then it was on to Oyster Bay Chickee. There, we were under a mosquito attack all night. Nobody could set up a tent because with such a big group, there's not room. And I learned that night that the mosquitoes come both ways. They settle down from above and they also come up through the cracks in the chickee.

We wore head nets and got in the sleeping bags. Hot as the devil in there. And, of course, when the net would get against your face, they'd bite right through it. Early in the morning a front goes through, rain and wet and lightning. But we went on to South Joe Chickee, and at South Joe that night, huge electrical storm. Winds got sixty knots, things blowing off the chickee. Mike Regner had set up a hammock between two posts, and the wind blew him out over the water and he's yelling, "Help me! Help me!" The boats are banging, and Lou and I are securing boats. One guy's kayak got caught underneath the chickee, so we're trying to get that boat free, waves coming in. It was miserable. Absolutely miserable.

Next morning, five of the group said, "Enough is enough. We don't want to continue. We can paddle into Flamingo from South Joe."

I said, "I wouldn't recommend it. The winds are up from the southeast, still gusting to thirty knots. You can get along the edge and maybe hang in, but then you go through the canal into Coot Bay and that's going to be rugged." But Al Harrington and Kurt Volker, they're really experienced people, said they would go and look after the group. So they left.

For us, the next night's destination was Hells Bay Chickee, so we had to get across Whitewater Bay. The problem with Whitewater is winds come up in the southeast, and they build from the lower part. If you're up in the Watson River, tricky area, you can look down and see the end of Whitewater Bay, and I've actually watched the waves get bigger and bigger as they come up. But Lou and I worked out a plan, how to skip across Whitewater Bay, hiding behind keys so we would just have short distances.

We went up Nomans River, and in the afternoon, we found the Hells Bay Chickee. Beautiful night. I said, "Those people just missed out."

At 3:00 in the morning another front comes through and Ruth Black's kayak is whanging against the chickee. So Lou and I are out, 3:00 in the morning in underwear, soaking wet, finally got the kayak up on the chickee. There's room now because there's only six of us. And, of course, in the morning everything was wet.

Worst trip I ever made. Virginia said, "Never, never again." And the group that left had a terrible trip in. Took them almost eight hours. They were afraid they would capsize. And if they weren't strong canoeists, you know, experienced, they would have been in trouble.

That was a '93 trip. I had done the Waterway before, in 1990. Ken was leading. He was paddling with Dean Sims who helped lay out the Wilderness Waterway. And we had a really interesting man, Art Ives, a retired army colonel and an Iroquois Indian, one of the best flatwater paddlers I have ever seen. He had that feather shaped paddle and did the underwater recovery. He'd make a beautiful long stroke, and then he'd put the paddle parallel to the canoe, slide it back, and the paddle never came out of the water.

I was paddling with Nancy Christensen, an experienced outdoor person, but she had never done the Waterway, just dreamed of doing it. We had a good Everglades paddler, Bill Hays, and he was paddling with Don, who'd been a Boy Scout leader. In all, it was a good group of twelve people.

We stopped at Lopez for lunch the first day, then went on to Watsons Place, twelve miles. Next day Lostmans. There's nice swimming up Lostmans River if you go up the river a way where water is not quite as salty. A lot of those little jellyfish were there.

Then, at Broad River, got up early to do the Nightmare. I'm in the first canoe, and Nancy's up front, and there's a mangrove tree uprooted and down across the channel. Now, I had a whitewater canoe, flat bottom, so I go right over it, but as we were going over, I jumped out. I said, "There's no way that Bill Hayes in that big Grumman is going to get over this. I'll have to help him."

The canoes were coming on, and one by one we pulled them over the downed tree. Bill Hayes turns out to be last, and we were in that marl/muck clear to my waist, but we finally got that big Grumman over. I'm covered with muck clear to my elbow.

That night we made it all the way up the Harney River, across Tarpon Bay to Avocado Creek and then to Canepatch. It was an absolutely gorgeous camp site, a big shell mound. It was pre—Hurricane Andrew, so the avocado trees were still there and the orange trees and bananas. But I'm still covered with mud. I say to Art, "I'm jumping out of the canoe right into the water. You watch those gators across there." And so I jump in, clothes and all, and I pop up in the water nose to snout with a big old alligator! Art, he's a cartoonist, said, "I've never saw anyone just bolt out of the water and end up on the dock like that!"

By the time you get up to Canepatch, the water's salt content is low, but it's not drinkable. But do you know at the turn of the twentieth-century sailors used to stop and fill water barrels at the mouth of the Harney River? Those cargo transports, schooners, would go from Ft. Myers to Key West, and they'd fill water barrels at the mouth of the Harney River. That water is salty now.

The next day, Dean Sims was tired. He had been cramping, and he was suffering. Winds were really up, but we had a tailwind. So we tied my canoe to his, lashed 'em together. He had a tarp, so Nancy held her paddle up and tied the tarp to it. We sailed, *shoosh*, down Tarpon Bay and down the Shark River.

We were at Oyster Bay that night, so the next day we had to cross Whitewater Bay. I was telling everybody, "I know the winds. We have to get up early. We gotta get out of here." I said, "Look, we'll go across to the North River. It's the shortest crossing,

about five miles. And we've got some keys up there to hide behind before we have to cross the open water."

So we start out together, and all of a sudden Ken is veering off, and I called at Dean, "Where you guys going?"

Nancy panicked, "You've got to follow Ken. Got to follow Ken."

I said, "Ken doesn't know where he's going." But I gave up, followed Ken, got up to him and said, "Look, you guys are going wrong."

Alligator with mosquitos. Photograph by Anne McCrary Sullivan.

"No, no, no we're not wrong."

It was pure luck that we found the Roberts River. Ken saw the manatee sign. That gave him a key, you know. I asked, "What is wrong?"

Dean said, "I just went by the compass."

"Then there's something wrong with that compass."

It turns out, Ken always carried a big magnet. At the chickees, he would fish for his Swiss Army knife that he lost three years ago at some chickee. So the compass is sitting on top the food bucket, and underneath that food bucket is a big magnet throwing off the compass.

At Roberts River Chickee we had some fun. That afternoon, the women on the trip came up to me and said, "Bill, do you still have those oranges and grapefruits?" I always carry a bag of them, just tie them in a net sack. I said, "Yeah, I've got a few left."

"Can we have them?"

"Alright. It's the last night. You can have them."

They had been teased, especially by Don, about how all those long paddles were going to build their upper body parts. So they went into the restroom and came out with a grapefruit and an orange in their shirts. That was after somebody got a big pot and mixed up all Dean Sims's cordials. He had cleaned out his liquor cabinet of cordials, brought them all on the trip. And somebody had a mix, powdered grapefruit or something, so they mixed it all up, and we all dipped in with a Sierra cup or something.

It was calm the next morning down the Roberts River. There's nothing more beautiful than going down the Roberts with the sun coming up and the moon setting. And Whitewater Bay was like glass. We glided across Coot Bay Pond, down the Buttonwood and home. That was my first trip. We didn't struggle with bad weather. Nancy got to go, and, yeah, it was a good trip.

The last trip I made through the Wilderness Waterway was just Mike Thompson and Dave Young and me. Neither one of them had done it, and they asked me if I'd be interested in leading them through. I jumped at the opportunity. It was the best trip I ever made. One of the highlights of that trip, for me, was going down the Rodgers River. I had never been down the Rodgers, and it was great going down that river, an absolutely beautiful day, rough coming into the bay, but we saw porpoises right up next to the boat. I have a note from Dave thanking me for inviting him on that trip, said "Bill, you and Mike are the best paddling partners. I'd follow your group anywhere. Loop trip next year."

Since then I've made several loop trips, including one around the Capes. We saw loggerheads going up the Shark River. I remembered one time Virginia and I saw

some huge loggerheads. The jellyfish were coming out of the Shark Valley Slough into the bay, and that's what the loggerheads feed on. They would rise by the canoe, I mean close, right by the canoe. "I hope they don't hit this canoe, those big old things."

I've been out to Alligator Creek a lot. I led a group out to clear the whole trail after Hurricane Andrew. There were twelve of us and one of the things we had to do was clear out Shark Point. The Park Service won't let us use chain saws because there's no help if somebody gets hurt out there, so we have to use hand tools. They let us use a weed whacker. But it was so funny trying to get out of the canoe anywhere close to Shark Point. You'd be full of mosquitoes. So Bill Lynch got all his rain gear on and head net, gloves. We dropped him off with a weed eater and then went offshore to get away from the mosquitoes. We heard the trimmer start up, "*Broom, broom, brr, puh, puh, puh, puh, puh . . .*" Shut down. We came back. It had clogged up, the intake full of mosquitoes.

Years later I was out there with my neighbor and we hiked down to the point. It was beautiful. And the warblers were migrating through there. You've got some blow-downs and things from storms, but it was wonderful.

Old Plate Creek Chickee. Built on the pilings of a former land development office, the spacious old Plate Creek Chickee was a favorite for many paddlers eager to stretch their legs and spread out a little. It has now been replaced by a smaller chickee, but remnants of the original building remain visible nearby. Photograph by Holly Genzen.

Rainbow over mangroves. Photograph by Anne McCrary Sullivan.

PART III

IN ALL KINDS OF WEATHER: KAYAK AND FOLBOT

EVERY TRIP IS THE TRIP OF A LIFETIME

Rick Horton

KAYAKER

About twenty-five years ago, knowing my fascination for charts and my predisposition for daydreaming, my wife, Pauline, gave me a set of nautical charts that covered the area in and about Everglades National Park. It was the perfect gift. I have spent countless hours poring over the thousands of miles of interconnected waterways, bays, and the labyrinth of mangrove islands known collectively as the Ten Thousand Islands. The names and places of islands and homesteads become a South Florida kayaker's rosary, each island a small bead gently caressed by the mind and eye. Turtle Key, Lumber, Rabbit, and Crate. . . . I can recite them by memory all the way to Flamingo. Such is the legacy of a misspent adulthood.

Sweetwater was the first chickee that I ever spent the night on. It was summer. Water was touching the two-by-six that the chickee sits on. So I just lift myself up and put my bum on the chickee. I turn around and there're ten alligators behind me. I don't know where they came from because they weren't there when I paddled up. They're all looking at me. I'm thinking, "Someone's been feeding them. They're habituated." I am looking at the measly six inches separating me from the expectant reptiles, especially the big guy, and I'm thinking that this chickee stuff might not be such a good idea.

Do alligators sun on these chickees? If I was an alligator, I would because there are no banks for me to lie on. So what happens at night? Do they crawl out at night?"

As usual, insects force me into my tent at 6:30 p.m. Sun doesn't go down until 8:30, and I'm layin' on my little sleeping pad, just layin' there and sweating, and I'm lookin' out and the gators are still there, still waiting to see if I'm going to give them some food, I guess.

I don't know when it was, but I fell asleep and then I wake up to this thrashing. I look out and I can't see anything. I hear a lot of moving out there, but I don't see anything. And then I hear dolphin

Fog at Sweetwater Creek. Photograph by Holly Genzen.

*Hog Key Royal Poinciana.
Photograph by Rick Horton.*

breathing. Dolphins had chased mullet up into that little bay and were feeding voraciously. I figured Flipper never would have let an alligator attack Bud, right? And I fell back into some sort of exhausted state of slumber.

Now, I've seen dolphin feed like that numerous times. I know they will often bite like the filet mignon out of a mullet, leave the head and tail. Are the alligators there picking up the pieces? I think they are. I think the alligators learned long ago that this is where a free meal comes from.

I read Charlton Tebeau's *The Story of Chokoloskee Bay Country* recently and am amazed at how short a time white settlers have been down in these parts. I would have thought 1810–20s rather than 1870s. Most of the homesites were inhabited and abandoned within sixty years or less. I am fascinated by the picture of the cistern Tebeau photographed at Turner River, which has to have been taken after 1947. It is a mature mangrove forest now and was the first time I paddled by it in 1992. Forty-five years from flat shell, soil field, to saltwater forest. It is hard to fathom.

On the Halfway Creek loop, Tebeau was right, look for the poinciana trees and you'll find some of the old homesites. I found a cane mill by one set of poincianas. The big flywheel motor that ran it is on the creek bank. I would imagine that back then a lot of the mangroves we see now were not even there. Darwin's Place was willows, and when he lived there, it was all fresh water. That's how he grew his vegetables. You look at other places like Farm Creek, it's not called Farm Creek because they wanted to farm there, it's because they *did* farm there.

I think the amount of fresh water pouring down from the north was so huge before the Tamiami Trail was built, before Disston started anything north of

Okeechobee, that it was radically different. If we could go back 150 years, we would not recognize it.

I can't recall any trip down in the Everglades that has not been memorable. I remember one night I spent on South Lostmans. It was a summer day, windy, and when I get to the beach I look northeast and see an enormous squall line. Soon the wind is howling, the lightning crashing, and rain is in driving waves. My rain fly is leaking like a sieve. You have to take the good with the bad, and I figure this isn't so bad; I could be outside trying to paddle or even trying to survive.

In the morning I wake to find the world washed clean. Looking about the small island of South Lostmans, I feel as if I am the only person on the planet. That is part of the definition of wilderness: that there be little or no evidence of a lasting impact made by man. Not much of the Everglades will fall under that definition, but South Lostmans did that morning.

Another memorable summer trip, I was crossing Ponce de Leon Bay, watching a huge thunderhead build up over Whitewater Bay. I cruise past the tip of Shark River Island, lightning flashing, thunder rolling, sticking close to the mangroves for a little safety, but the mangroves sit on a four-foot-high clay bank, and when the waves crash into the bank, they reflect some of the energy back at me. It's like paddling in a Maytag washing machine.

There were two lonely cabbage palms at that end of Northwest Cape, and when I saw them, you would have thought I had seen my salvation. When I got to the beach, I dragged the boat up and just kind of huddled there waiting the storm out. The storm passed by in about an hour. So I pulled the boat up into the grass and camped there, right at that very top end of Northwest Cape, by the palms. When the storm winds left, the bugs ventured back to the beach. I retired to my tent where I had a reservation for one at Chez Rick. They serve a remarkable peanut butter and jelly sandwich, and the dessert cart has cookies!

I got up before dawn and sat in the tent in the dark, ate my breakfast. I always take what I call a "night bottle" so I don't have to go outside when there are a lot of bugs. Six inches away from my head there's this boiling mass of insects and it's like, I'm not going out. I'll have breakfast, get my gear all bagged up, and then open the tent.

I can see where turtles came ashore to lay eggs. Their flippers leave distinctive tractor tread marks in the sand. I look out to the Gulf just as a four-foot tarpon launches itself into a graceful arc, leaping three feet fully clear of the water.

It was in that early gloaming that I'm paddling down Northwest Cape. I'm thinking it is such a beautiful morning it would be sacrilegious to make any noise in this place. Ahead, I see a grove of black mangroves sanded in by some storm. And what should I see wending its way through the trees but a Florida panther. I stop paddling, my eyes riveted on the big cat. It doesn't see me. When it gets almost abreast of the boat, it notices me and stops to watch. As I drift past, it crouches as though to spring away but doesn't. We watch each other for another twenty seconds and then with a bound it vanishes into marsh grasses behind the trees.

I continue down to Middle Cape. At first I think I see a person or a small boat on the beach. As I get closer it dawns on me that I'm looking at yet another endangered creature that calls the 'Glades home. It's an American crocodile, about eight feet long. As soon as it sees the boat, it's up and off the beach. As one of three hundred or so, it is a good find, not as good as the panther but I'll take it. The croc swims a little ways from shore and I pass between it and the beach. I have seen many alligators, but this is only my third croc and my best viewing by far. Even though you might think the croc sees me as food, it is more likely that it perceives me as a nineteen-foot predator gliding through its territory. I don't think it knows yet that a kayak is crunchy on the outside and chewy on the inside. Let's hope that it never does. I think I'll refrain from swimming at Middle Cape.

This is the day I will go down to Flamingo, call Pauline, pick up some more drinking water and come back to East Cape to camp for the night. As I turn the corner at East Cape, I feel a breeze start up out of the southwest. It gives me a little push down to Flamingo.

The Park Service doesn't recommend summer camping mainly because of the bugs, but if you want the place to yourself, summer is the time to do it. For the three days I was at Cape Sable there wasn't another soul for thirty miles camping or walking the beach.

After sunset the number of stars that are visible is amazing. In the wintertime you could lie out on the beach and really enjoy them. As it is, I pay for my stargazing by spending the next half hour killing bugs that hitched a ride into the tent. I fall asleep wondering just where exactly crocodiles sleep at night.

I wake up before sunrise and see close together a thin sliver of a crescent moon and a planet in the eastern horizon. I am in no hurry this morning because I plan no more than about fifteen miles today. The next night will be back at Northwest Cape. I paddle leisurely up to Middle Cape and see the crocs again. They were in the water watching me.

I make camp early, about 1:30 p.m. I eat lunch and then go for a walk down the beach, almost all the way back to the Middle Cape Canal. I come across a number of new turtle nests. It's about a 50/50 split as to the number raided by raccoons and those left undisturbed. I see a raccoon ahead on the beach, up by the grass line. I watch as it works its way past me. It stops to check out a new turtle nest, digging tentatively in a few places, but then moves on. I imagine that turtle mortality is very high.

I walk by the water's edge swishing my feet through the water to cool down a bit. Except for the two palms back by the tent there is no shade down on the beach. No wonder there are no other campers. Torrid heat and endless swarms of ravening insects.

Morning breaks once more on Cape Sable. There is not a breath of wind outside the tent. I get loaded up, and by 6:45 a.m. I'm heading back up the coast in conditions the complete opposite of when I came down. As I go across the cove at Big Sable Creek there are tarpon rolling all over the place. All those big game fish and not a fisherman in sight. Up ahead I see what looks like a fog bank just past Shark River Island. I smell smoke and I realize there must be a large fire either in the Everglades or Big Cypress. At Shark River Island the smoke is so thick I can't even see the three miles to Shark Point and Graveyard Creek. The names kind of make you think . . . Shark River, Shark River Island, Shark Point, Graveyard Creek. Is there something here they aren't telling us? I take a compass heading for Shark Point and start paddling. Ponce de Leon Bay is glass calm.

I see an eagle before heading up Broad Creek. I go into the Nightmare, but after my third dead-end passage I say forget this and paddle back the way I came. The reason it's called the Nightmare is because you get nightmares thinking about spending the night in there. Soon I am gliding past Highland Point and then the abandoned ranger's station at Lostmans River. Past a few more points of land I see the poinciana tree on Hog Key (see photo on page 112). The tree is blooming, and this remains the prettiest spot on the whole trip.

It is now 6:15 in the morning. It is just light enough for me to make out a cloud of no-see-ums in front of the tent. Last night the raccoons were so noisy it made sleep almost impossible. They just could not leave the kayak alone. In the beginning I was able to scare them off by yelling and growling, but later on they came back and stayed. I looked out the door and I could see a coon on the front of the boat. The starlight made it easy to watch, and what the coon was doing was licking dew off the boat. I would imagine if fresh crab legs are a big part of your diet you might work up a thirst by the end of the day.

I head for a small sand spit just before Mormon Key and stop for lunch. I always keep a bag in front of my feet that has my paddle jacket, my bug gear, food. I have a little plastic can of trail mix, some Slim Jims, and always a good supply of cookies.

Pauline makes a great lemon cookie that travels well, and I try to take five dozen or so. Armies have failed and empires crumbled because of a lack of good homemade cookies. I bring nothing to cook. That's just me. I never got into coffee or tea.

With it being Saturday there are a jillion boats with fisher folk on them but that's all right. I had my week. I set a compass course for Duck Rock and shoot a straight course across Chatham Bend. It is still quite calm, and I would like to make as much headway as possible before the sea breeze starts.

I see dolphin and turtle again in Rabbit Key Pass. The wind picks up by the time I reach Chokoloskee Bay. Just two miles of whitecaps separate me from the end of my journey. I hesitated at first to call this a trip of a lifetime until I realized that no matter how many times I did this trip again it would never be exactly the same. Every trip is a trip of a lifetime. For that matter, every day is a day of a lifetime, never to be reclaimed once it's gone. We should greet each day for what it is, one day out of a finite number of days that grows increasingly smaller each sunrise.

My memory of things which do not interest me is quite poor. Unfortunately, much of what I have done during my life seems to fall into this category. But my memory of things that took place on or in the water is very good . . . several meetings with dolphins where they come up and gaze at me with that unblinking jet-black eye as if to say, "I am curious, who are you? What are you? Will you play with me?" The time Pauline and I saw two dolphins, one sighted and the other blind—its eyes white and completely opaque—with the sighted one gently guiding the blind one by nudging its snout under the other's chin. The roseate spoonbills I drifted under while riding the incoming tide into the pass at Rodgers River. The immature laughing gull I paddled up to and brought into the boat to remove fishing line and hook from its wing, which then sat on my kayak and regarded me with its jet bead eye as if to try and understand what has just taken place. The laughing gull that held my eye on the bay of Ponce de Leon, wondering why I would be there in such adverse conditions. The star fields at night and me wondering at my proper place in all of this immensity.

Also memorable but for different reasons . . . the osprey hanging dead in the black mangrove with the shiny fishing lure through its taloned foot and the line wrapped in the branches, its mate sitting on another branch calling. How many days did it take for the first bird to die, trying to fly and not being able, finally hanging upside down? The hawksbill turtle found dead on the beach with the marks of an improperly functioning turtle excluder crushed into its carapace. How long did a

Graveyard Creek.
Photograph by Rick Horton.

creature that can hold its breath for hours last in the throat of the net with tons of catch piling on top?

But the trip that has left the most indelible memories was a trip that I chose to take with no books, no MP3 player, phone, or electronic devices. I even chose not to keep a trip journal. I wanted to spend ten days by myself just listening to the wilderness. I wanted to really try to see the interconnection between the natural elements and this wonderfully harsh environment that calls to me so deeply. Even now, if I close my eyes and calm my mind, I can recall almost every paddle stroke with amazing clarity. Each encounter with a bird, fish, reptile or mammal, of trees, and even a particular insect or two. I believe this is possible for anyone, and is possible anywhere, although for me it is much easier in a wilderness area such as the Everglades.

For me to be able to focus my full attention requires that I have no distractions, and I am easily distracted. Even another person on the trip is a distraction. There are times when a simple joy that is shared with others is multiplied manifold. But there are also times when a small secret joy must be held close to your heart, to be cherished by you alone. A solo wilderness experience will freely give you a thousand secret gifts. It becomes a multiday mindful meditation where objects and events take

on a new and a greater, more powerful meaning. The more you observe, the more you focus on each new gift that Nature has left for you to find, the more such gifts you will find.

The great blue heron on an oyster bar on the way to Rabbit Key Pass, the empty crown conch shell at New Turkey campsite, the dolphin feeding vigorously in Wood Key Cove, the perfect spoonbill feather I found at low tide at Hog Key, the sawfish hunting on the shallow flats off Highland Beach, a loggerhead turtle catching a breath of air in front of a cathedral of old red mangroves; lying on the Shark River Chickee watching a yellowed red mangrove leaf fall from the tree and slowly drift by on the ebb of the tide beginning its own uncertain journey of discovery, listening to the breeze in the buttonwoods at Lane Bay Chickee; the io moth caterpillar in Whitewater Bay—all of these and countless others were the gifts I received.

I had understood on an intellectual level that all of Nature is an interwoven fabric, but this trip allowed me to *feel* the fabric, even if it was just a couple of threads of weft and warp. This has not led to much of an understanding of my place in this world, but it is enough that I am confident in the knowledge that my thread in the tapestry is over- and underlapped by many threads, both seen and unseen, and I am inextricably bound to Nature.

There is a song of redemption that Nature sings for us, and once you have heard it, even a part of it, it will remain with you, a small calm oasis in your heart and mind that will help you as you continue life's journey in our world.

Daydreaming is a great pastime of mine. The mind wanders down the corridors where memories are kept, and most of my fondest memories involve water that tastes of salt and air that is scented with sea grass and mangroves, mudflats, and oyster bars. It is a smell that comforts me and tells me I am home, that I have come back to my true home. My body desires a physical challenge. And my soul fills with a wanderlust that threatens to overwhelm and burst me if not allowed out. So I look at nautical charts that I've marked with all the places I've been and all the many more places I have not. Gradually a plan forms, although it is more like fermentation, for this is the most intoxicating part of the trip. What will I see when I journey into the wilderness? What wonders or mysteries will unveil themselves? And will I allow myself to become open enough to perceive them?

For me time spent alone in the wilderness is a time of spiritual redemption. To make myself whole again; and when I am whole (at least more whole than when I started) I am simply happier and more content with myself and the world around me. I believe this endeavor to restore ourselves must be done alone. A solo trip to the wilderness is a way to disengage, to unplug yourself from this modern life and go on a search. You might be surprised what you will find.

A GUIDE'S-EYE VIEW

John Lewis

KAYAK TOUR GUIDE

This morning was a gorgeous day. We started out on open ponds and lakes and then went into the maze of tunnels on the East River. We got into a tunnel so narrow between prop roots and branches that we had to take our kayak paddles apart and use them as canoe paddles. Finally, we just used our hands and went through laying down in the boat because branches were just on top of our heads. It was like the hands-on feeling was another sense, in addition to sight, sound, and smell. Once you start touching those prop roots and branches, then you really feel you're immersed in the Everglades.

I'm from Michigan, so I'm just down here during the winter months. This is my eleventh season in the Everglades. I love the biological diversity here and the weather, of course. I've worked with Ivey House about nine years. They offer "Everglades Adventures," which is their outdoor division of canoe and kayak rentals and guided trips. We do a lot on the Turner River. Because of the very small elevational change in the Everglades, sometimes a foot to two feet can change the ecosystem, unlike out west where it might take five thousand feet to go from one ecosystem to the other. So we can go into places like the Turner River and see three different ecosystems within a six-mile paddle. We can start in the freshwater bald cypress ecosystem and then go into the mangrove estuary and end up in a sawgrass prairie.

I decided to do the East River with this morning's group because of water levels now and the amount of wildlife we're seeing. The East River has a rookery this time of year. It has tricolored herons and snowy egrets in breeding plumage, which typically we only see three or four weeks, when they're right in the midst of attracting mates. And then there are the alligators, although because it is brackish water the concentration of alligators is not as great as in freshwater.

Typically, in the evenings, we go out before sunset, watch twilight, transition, and then put on headlamps and come back through the tunnels at night, kind of an eerie experience, not something you would think of doing on your own. The East River gives us lots of tunnels, lots of maze. So, just like trail hiking, we're going to the next intersection, regrouping, and making sure everyone is there. Then we do a kind of leapfrogging, to make sure that we keep everyone collected together. If you've

Mangroves at Little Shark River. Photograph by Anne McCrary Sullivan.

paddled out through the Ten Thousand Islands area in the daytime, you can imagine going through that process at night.

One of the unique things about the Everglades is the reflections as you paddle through these passages. It is a landscape painting unfolding in front of you, a Monet painting, if you will. And if you're the first kayaker, that mirror image has not got a ripple on it. It almost looks like the tunnel dead-ends because of that painting unfolding in front of you. Once that second, third, and fourth kayak comes, those boats are creating ripples. Also, you're seeing the kayaks ahead of you. It's a totally different image. So we rotate through the front. I think it's really special to be able to lead so I'll always work at everybody having a chance to experience (if they feel comfortable) leading through the tunnels.

A lot of the wildlife is very hard to see. I talk about how you're either a predator or you're prey, and you have a tendency to want to be camouflaged. If you're a predator, you don't want what you're feeding on to see you. If you're prey, you don't want that predator to see you. So little green herons, you can literally be ten feet away from 'em and looking and you won't pick them out, because they're sitting there fishing—what I call stalking—frozen in position waiting for a minnow to come underneath so they can grab it. The green herons blend in perfectly with the landscape.

As guides, we have to adapt to different people with lots of varied backgrounds, so we get to feel the nuances of people and change the itinerary for them or look for different things. Where you get only two people on your trip and they're birders and from Great Britain, they're happy to just sit in the boat, look at the warblers in the canopy and maybe not paddle a half-mile. But it's hard when you have tremendous variation in a group. If you've got ten people that have totally different backgrounds or interests, then it's more challenging. I find as a whole, though, when you get a big group, they start interacting and finding out about where they're from and what their interests are, and it actually works out really well.

When I have two hard-core paddlers and also some families that are less inclined to paddle fast, I'll say, "Okay, Sam, Mary, why don't you go over and see where that tunnel leads or see what's in that next lake over to the side?" They can go out and paddle and then be in a little bit of solitude and I can still have contact with them in sight distance, but they aren't sitting there with that group of ten people.

As guides we're responsible for everybody on the water, and as long as we can do the paddle safely, we are going out there. If there's lightning or if there's some type of risk, then we have the discretion of saying, "Okay. We're not going to paddle today because the risk is too great." Typically for us that's not a problem 'cause we're protected doing the interior. In more open water, exposed, the risk is a little greater.

When groups go out, there are usually more single kayaks than tandems. We recommend singles, believe it or not, because in a single kayak it's an easier learning curve; you're not trying to find those paddling partner nuances, when they're

Great egret and snowy egret.
Photograph by Anne McCrary
Sullivan.

Evening clouds, Lane Bay. Photograph by Anne McCrary Sullivan.

zigging and you're supposed to be zagging. But that eight- to twelve-year-old has to be in the front of a tandem with his parents just because of size. And you have a lot of people that are just apprehensive being in a boat by themselves. Today I had ten people and four were in tandems and the other six were in singles. And sometimes we do feel like we're a mommy duck with our ducklings organized and keeping them out of trouble.

I sometimes get people calling from Europe and the US, wanting to do the Wilderness Waterway or come paddling for seven or ten days, and I'm saying, "On the interior path, the Wilderness Waterway, there's not a lot of places to get out of your boat. You're in your boat from morning to night. That's one of the reasons I like a lot of exterior paddling as well as interior. You can do things like chickees and then you can do ground sites and historical places like Watson's, and then some beach sites for western sunsets and to walk the beach. The big advantage of the interior is it's so much more protected. Even the bigger bays like Oyster Bay can get choppy and rough but not impossible.

As a whole, people are apprehensive about two things in the Everglades—alligators and being lost. Going on a guided trip gives you some level of confidence. You have people with experience paddling around alligators and you learn that the American alligator is what we call an opportunist, not aggressive. The American alligator's meal is predominately fish and it's lunchbox sized, small. We're too big to be a food source. But the story and movie industry has a tendency to embellish. It's not a great movie if you're not tipped over and attacked by an alligator.

The Turner River is my favorite spot to paddle anywhere in North America. You will see more in three hours there in roughly a small area than you will most trips of seven or ten days because the biological diversity is immense in there with those three different ecosystems. Unfortunately, we've done a tremendous amount of promoting that area. It's in places like, "1000 Things to See or Do Before You Die." If you go to Fodor's guide and look in the Everglades, it's going to be "Paddling the Turner River." Needless to say, that's brought in more people. We're starting to say, "Okay, what's the carrying capacity for paddlers in there?" It's changing the atmosphere of the paddling experience because you're not going to paddle the Turner River and find solitude. There's going to be other people there.

The Turner River has a good variety of orchids. Most of them are blooming in August. Typically, we're not doing the kayak trips then because of the heat, the humidity, and the lightning storms, which are creating usable nitrogen for orchids, which need extra energy for flowering and creating seeds during that period of time.

Typically, the orchids that we're familiar with are hybrids. If you go to a flower ship and buy a corsage, that's going to be a hybrid, larger and more showy. A lot of the orchids here are small and epiphytic, growing up in the tree canopy, so they don't have soil for moisture and nutrients. They obtain all that from out of the sky.

The orchid family is one of the biggest families of plants and it's found on every continent except for Antarctica. There are so many unique flower arrangements and adaptations. Like the ghost orchid is specifically trying to attract a sphinx moth, so it's a night pollinator. There's one here called the night-scented orchid, gives scent off at night to attract that sphinx moth that has an extra long proboscis that can go down in this long conical flower looking for nectar and pollinating. And a lot of those orchids are specifically adapted with what I call a "landing pad" for that insect to land on to pollinate it.

Some of the mangrove tunnels are short. The alligators come into these tunnels at night because they've learned if they go in the tunnel twenty feet and face out, as the fish go from this lake to the next lake, they are funneled right to them. That alligator just lays there waiting for a fish dinner. The fish come right to him. So again, alligators are opportunists.

So the other night I'm leading a paddle, four people, and we're coming through these tunnels. I've got a tandem couple from Switzerland in front, pretty good paddlers, and as we're coming through there, the girl in the front says, "I felt an alligator bump under my feet." Then he comes up right beside the boat. They've got a fourteen-and-a-half-foot boat and this gator looks as long as their boat. And of course, they're frozen. I'm four feet behind them, saying "Keep paddling! Keep paddling! Keep paddling!" The two kayakers and the boat were probably 400 pounds and the alligator was probably 250 pounds, so he's not really interested in harming them. They just kind of spooked him a little bit. Normally when you do that they're just going to kick their tail and take off. But it was mating season. I'm thinking maybe he was, "Okay, I'm a lovey-dovey. This is another female and I want to push up against her." I'm like, "Forget the gator. Forget the gator. Watch where you're going. Paddle on your left. Paddle on your left" because if you paddle on the right you'd actually hit his back. Finally, I take the tail of their boat and shove it on by. So, all kinds of experiences.

Sleeping mudbound with tricolored heron. Photograph by Ann Rougle.

BECAUSE IT WAS GLORIOUS TO JUST KEEP SAILING

Ann Rougle

FOLBOT SAILOR AND PARK VOLUNTEER

Journal: South Joe River. Day One.

Late afternoon on South Joe Chickee. I am in a bay off the Joe River, on a wooden platform. Water surrounds me. There are no sounds but those of wind and water and sea creatures. My boat is secured for the night. Dinner has been cleared away. It is still light, and the mosquitoes who live in the mangroves that ring this bay have not yet found me, so I linger outside my tent, reveling in the breeze, the evening sun, the chatter of the water beneath me. I am alone and I am joyful. I smile silent thanks to the Park Service for building these shelters for folks like me, who love to travel the watery world of Everglades National Park.

There is fish noise all night. Schools of tiny creatures froth the surface as some bigger hungry guy rises from the bottom, picking off the danglers who can't get airborne in time. The sound is startling, like sudden surf.

Journal: Day Two.

I waited for the sun to rise, then sailed through the Joe River's many twists and turns, I saw dolphins fishing at every point of land, their fins cutting figure-eights like snorkelers circling a coral fan. I stopped for a break at the Joe River Chickee. So did two motorboats. The people were friendly, curious. "What kind of boat is that?" Already, on Day Two, I am in solitary mode. The request to enter into conversation pulls against the grain. I answer in monosyllables, leave quickly, drawn away by the tug of the wind in the sail.

I started sailing going on sixty years ago now. But then life took a turn, and I had a long, boatless dry spell. I didn't get on the water for decades and decades, seemed like.

My final job had me living in a cubicle, pager on the hip, on call twenty-four hours a day. When it came time to retire, I decided I was going to need a hobby. I bought a clarinet at a yard sale and signed up for lessons. Somehow, that didn't work out for me real well. Clarinets have these cantankerous reeds. Yeah, the reeds were the problem, that's it.

Next, I tried kayaking. I went on a two-hour tour in Key West, and the minute I sat in that cheap old plastic kayak and was floating on water again, it brought back my childhood love of water all in a rush. I was hooked. Driving home from Key West, I passed a kayak shop that had a nice little six-foot

Hazel at East Cape Beach.
Photograph by Ann Rougle Folbot.

kayak out front. That's perfect, thought I. I'll buy it and toss it into the back of the van, and we can travel the country together. So I went into the shop to buy it. And they said no. But, I said—I'm driving back to Maryland and I desperately need a kayak small enough for my van. That one is perfect. Again, no. They knew that as a total beginner I would not be happy in a tiny whitewater kayak, and even though they could have made a sale that day to an out-of-stater they'd never see again, they refused to do it. "We will sell you this magazine," they said. "Look at the article on folding kayaks." So they made all of two dollars from me that day. I went home, read the magazine, and ordered my first folder, a twelve-foot Folbot, and was happy as can be. I built a bed for me in the van and a spot for *Sir Lance* (that Folbot is the Aleut model. Sir Lance Aleut. Get it?), and we hit the road, driving all over the country looking for places to paddle. The clarinet stayed home.

One time, driving to Key West, I decided to take a right turn and stop in at Everglades National Park. It knocked my socks off. Everything about it was beautiful to me. It felt like home. The first trail I walked was the West Lake boardwalk through the mangroves. I'd never seen mangroves before, and here I was, walking through a jungle of arching prop roots and dangling aerial roots. I knew then that I had to find a way to paddle through the mangroves. I went on all the day-paddles I could find out of Flamingo, prowling through mangrove tunnels and exploring mangrove-ringed bays. I tried an overnight or two to nearby chickees. And that was it. I knew I needed to find a way to be out here for as long as possible.

My first cruising Folbot was *Hazel* (see photo on page 130), named after this wonderful miniature cow that escaped from the farm of a friend of mine. She just leapt off the end of the pickup truck and ran off. She lived in the wild for almost a year before they found her. So *Hazel* was the perfect name for this boat. And perfect she was—except for the thing about oysters.

Oysters are my biggest fear. I tremble in terror at the thought of Hypalon-slashing oyster beds. And snags. When you're sailing and the wind is shoving you right towards something scary and sharp, you can't just put on the brakes and back-paddle.

Everglades National Park is a designated wilderness area, but it's a wilderness area that permits motorboats. So for a while, I was timid about anchoring out, afraid of getting hit by a powerboat while I was sleeping at anchor. Permit problems finally forced the issue. I was supposed to stay at New Turkey Key one night. I had a permit, but I found it already occupied. There were families with little children playing in the sand, and I didn't have the heart to go say, "Look, you have to leave because I have the permit for tonight." I just turned *Hazel* around and decided, "Okay, this is the night I'll try out my shelter and sleep on my boat." The only place I could find on my chart that looked at all welcoming was Bird Key, a little lagoon-shaped island, where I'd be sheltered and hidden. It looked snug and safe.

The chart clearly showed that the lagoon inside the key would be high and dry at low tide, but there was plenty of water there right then, so I went in. I needed the security of being enclosed inside the mangrove walls. It should be a nice, soft, oozy bottom, right? When the tide went down, I would settle on nice squishy mud, right? So I tied up between a couple of mangrove trees near the shore and set up my netting shelter well before mosquito time.

As the tide began to go down, I noticed with a jolt that not only was water under the boat dropping fast, jagged things were starting to poke up out of the bay. Snags, waterlogged branches with clumps of live oysters on them, and dead oyster shells that just lurk around to get you. They were all over the place. "Oh, man! There could be some right under my boat!" At this point, my boat was still swinging a little bit. It hadn't actually picked the spot it was going to settle onto. So I leaned over the side

Clubhouse Beach, low tide.
Photograph by Holly Genzen.

with my trusty and indestructible Folbot paddle and felt under the boat to try to scope out the situation, and—ulp—there were definitely things there. Hard, jagged things.

I leaned over one side and started sweeping clumps out from under the boat with the paddle, throwing them far away. Then I leaned over the other side to do the same thing—and the boat shifted. Now I had to clear an even wider spot. This was not working. Finally, I hopped out, sank into six inches of mud, and continued the sweeping process, trying to get her settled in a safe spot. Before I was finished, she settled.

At this point, I only knew for sure that the aft half of the boat was safely on oyster-free muck. So for hours I sat hunched up at the back of the cockpit, afraid to put my weight anywhere else. Finally, I realized, what will be will be; I'll wake up with an oyster shell sticking up through my hull or I won't. I made dinner and went to bed.

I set my alarm for the wee hours. I didn't want to sleep through the 3:00 a.m. high tide and on into another low. When I woke up, *Hazel* was just starting to float with the rising tide. I wondered, "Would I know yet, given the three inches of closed-cell foam floorboards between me and the bottom, if there's a hole? Would I know if

I was sinking or not?" But sometimes you just have to decide to decide something for the sake of your sanity. So I decided to decide that the hull was still intact. At 3:00 a.m., with what I hoped was a safe margin of water between me and the evil clumps, I left Bird Key to spend the rest of the night paddling in deeper water.

Night-paddling in the Everglades, I have hallucinations. After-images of looming, arching mangrove roots appear before my eyes, and even though the chart tells me it's open water all around me, I see keys that aren't there. It was eerie, feeling surrounded by obstacles that I was pretty sure were not there. Or were they?? At one point, I heard the telltale *CLANK* of the rudder hitting an oyster shell, followed by the *CLANKETY CLANK* of the bow's metal strip against sharp shells. I pulled on my boots, leapt out, and shoved *Hazel* off to safety. All was well. Except for no sleep and a trailing cloud of Bird Key mosquitoes. I paddled 'til daylight and on to the next camping spot.

Journal: Rounding the point I find a graceful curve of sand that spills out northwards from the island and swoops around to the east and back upon itself, almost full circle, enclosing a heart-shaped lagoon. I land and walk to the center of the sandy point. This is it—the isle of my dreams! A sandy camping spot with waterfront on three sides, sunrise to the right, sunset to the left. I move ashore.

So this is my island home, on the edge of the Gulf. I have a beach for every breeze! If the southerly sea breeze is in charge, I relax in the shade of my tarp on a tiny south-facing pocket beach. Late in the day, when the wind follows the sun around to the southwest, I sit on West Beach and watch dusk arrive, while the breeze obligingly keeps hungry winged creatures corralled in the woods behind me. After dark, as the dying sea breeze relinquishes control to the northerly, I move to the curving northern sandspit (dubbed, in honor of one of the bits of hardware on my Folbot, "J Hook"), for a late supper. I pondered long and hard, searching for a name for my island. With nods equally to Cyril Ritchard and Ferris Bueller, it is Hook Key.

Hazel and I are blissfully stranded here for four hours out of every 12, while the bay behind the island dries out and becomes a gigantic buffet for ibises and herons. As the tide comes in and the mudflats begin to fill, a solo dolphin appears. He works the flats systematically, moving up and down the bay, leaving behind him a billow of silt. I imagine him daintily rooting out truffly nuggets.

Ashore, flocks of butterflies make the most of a field of succulents blooming in the sand. Occasionally a bald eagle drops in for a photo shoot, obligingly posing atop a leafless tree. At low tide, a bleached sea-turtle skeleton gleams in the sun off West Beach, looking like nothing so much as a gigantic petrified moth. On the shores of Heart Lagoon, fiddler crabs sidle about. Strange that they only sidle. Never frontle or backle.

Some days I laze the day away, wandering my islet, reading in the shade of my tarp. Sometimes I go for a day sail, exploring nearby keys. Each evening, as I sit watching the dusk, waiting for my dinner water to boil,

three pelicans fly overhead and cross the bay on the way to their nighttime roost. Jet black against the sunset,
their bodies cylindrical, their wings wagging up and down in perfect unison.

One of my favorite beach sites is Rabbit Key. Rabbit Key is a fine place for people like me who like to watch their feet as they walk. Because so much is happening right at your feet! Looking down, I started to notice funny-looking tracks, kind of smudgy drag marks, maybe an inch and a half wide. At the end of each of these sandy tracks was a sand-colored baby horseshoe crab. They were all over the place, weaving this way and that, their tracks crisscrossing. When they bumped into each other, they'd just turn and go the other way. Not a bad life lesson.

A special bonus to Rabbit Key is that long spit where the birds stand at low tide. When the water comes up and the spit gets smaller, the birds inch backwards, and as the tide rises higher, they move backwards some more, and backwards some more, until they are right next to the island. You can watch them all day.

I love the beach sites because if you stay a few days, or if you're lucky and get marooned, there's nothing to do but look around and take note of things you'd otherwise miss. You'll find yourself slowed down. The place sets the pace.

Generally, I don't care as much for ground sites, but Lard Can gave me excellent shelter one blustery night. With a fierce wind, twenty-five knots and gusting right in my face as I tried to sail up the Lane River, current against me, I was barely able to make headway as I tacked up the river to my destination, Lane Bay Chickee. I kept my eyes on the prize of a mug of hot chocolate at the end of the slog, only to find a canoe already moored at the chickee and a couple of guys on the chickee platform. Quick double-check. Yep, I had the permit for Lane Bay Chickee that night.

"Are you guys staying here?" They said, "Yeah, if the wind doesn't die down." Well, I knew the forecast, and the wind was not going to slacken for a couple of days. So I said "Okey-dokey," and on I went. It was still early in the day and now, what had been a struggle turned into an adventure, a challenge, something I could do that these two strapping men couldn't. They were stuck. But because of this wonderful boat I could keep going in these conditions. Let's see how far I can get! I sailed my way upwind from Lane Bay to Hells Bay.

At Hells Bay Chickee both platforms were unoccupied, and I thought I might take a chance, camp there. But there was always the chance that someone might come up from the fairly sheltered Hells Bay Trail. Somebody might really need to stay here. I sailed on to Pearl Bay Chickee and found it, too, unoccupied. But again, someone might need it. So I went on to Lard Can, which can accommodate four parties, so even if someone else came, there should be room for all.

Lard Can was all mine all night and quite sheltered from the south wind. But the flip side to that lack of wind—it was extremely buggy! So I used my huge hand-me-down bug suit from an XXXL friend of mine. I can put on this vast shirt, pull my hands in, and actually have a cup of hot chocolate and read a book inside. It's like having my own personal tent.

Scorched mussels, Last Huston Bay. Common along Florida coasts, scorched mussels (Brachiodontes exustus) attach themselves to mangrove roots, filtering plankton from the ebb and flow of the tides. Photograph by Holly Genzen.

Evening at Crooked Creek.
Photograph by Holly Genzen.

Once, when I stopped at Broad River ground site for the night, there were already two canoers there, and they had moored their boat at the lower dock. I had to tie up at the high platform, which had no ladder. It was low tide, and the dock was higher than my head as I stood in the boat, then clambered onto a rail, carrying one dry bag at a time and hurling each one up on deck. The guys came over and said, "Hi, can we help you?" I said, "You know, thank you so much. That's a really kind offer, but I'm trying to figure out how to do this myself. You know, what if you guys weren't here? So I'm putting myself through this exercise of trying to do it myself, but thank you so much." They seemed okay with that.

In the morning, I had to perform the whole process in reverse, and over they came thinking maybe by now she'd be willing to see reason. When one of them offered help, I again declined as politely as I could. He said, "Well, you're just a one-woman man, aren't you?" I don't think he meant it unkindly. I thought, "Yeah. A one-woman man. A foot in both worlds. What could be better than that?"

That's one thing I like about going solo. You don't get into this division of labor thing. If you have two people, it's just natural that the one with stronger muscles does the heavy work and the other one does the fine motor work. It works. But I like being able to do all of the stuff, figuring it out. If there is competence to be gained, it's all mine. The failures and lessons learned are mine too.

Weather is certainly a hazard out there, especially if hazardous weather is your favorite kind. One time I was sailing the Wilderness Waterway up to Everglades City, planning to take two weeks, then turn around and come back. But I had such a southerly breeze, I was just tearing through those bays—Dad's, Chevelier, Huston, all those. I didn't bother stopping to stay at the chickees I had reserved. I just kept sailing. It was glorious to just keep sailing. I got to the mouth of the Lopez River, four days early, and found myself staring at civilization—Chokoloskee. I thought, "Hmm. I could go into Everglades City and get my Hershey bar, stay in a motel, get a hot shower, have a restaurant meal. Or I could go out and explore the Ten Thousand Islands." I knew that the next night, which was Christmas night, a cold front was coming through. I thought, "What would be the very best way to spend Christmas if you knew a serious storm was coming through? Would you spend it in a motel room? Of course not. You'd sail out and camp in the Ten Thousand Islands."

I sailed out to Hook Key, set up my tent right out in the open on the sandy hook. I'm sitting in my tent, both doors open, watching clouds assemble to the north and west, massive white cumuli on the top of purply-black ones. Squalls race toward my island, trailing tentacles of darkness. The NOAA weather radio system is telling me that there could be significant storm surge. I'm watching out the back window of the tent as the water rises toward *Hazel*. Then, when I turn to look out the front, I can no longer see the far shore, only a solid black wall, and it was coming fast.

There was nothing to do except watch it come. When the rain started, I closed the front tent flap, looked out the back. *Hazel* was still there. Rain was horizontal, and lightning was flashing all over the place. How do you keep yourself safe in a lightning storm when you're out like this? I know you can't. I've been told, "Well, maybe if you sit on your Thermarest." So I folded it up into thirds and perched there, enjoying the show. It was the most beautiful of lightning shows. Water crept higher and higher and the lightning kept flashing, but I didn't get electrocuted, and my boat didn't float away.

I do have my limits when it comes to weather. I've been scared by—a cloud. One time I launched from Flamingo for East Cape knowing there was a cold front coming. The thing about launching into a cold front is that nobody else will be out there.

Fishermen aren't out there. They're smarter than that. Me, the day that's forecast to have an evening cold front, that's my launch day. I want to be on Cape Sable with a front row seat, watch the storm come through, and then be stuck there for as long as possible. It's not smart, it's not prudent, and it's not recommended, but it's what I do.

This particular time, I put my tent a little bit inland, behind some thick bushes. I had heard that this cold front would be fast and furious, with possible tornadic activity. So I was standing on the beach, watching this cloud come racing at me. It was so low that it was sweeping the water. It was dark and seemed to have solid form. It was a wall of blackness, and I was terrified. I ran from the cloud and hid in my tent, even though I knew that a tent would not save me. I thought the cloud was going to kill me. I was a little kid again, terrified of the monster in the basement.

Normally I love nothing more than a good marooning. I have been known to design my trip so that I have a good chance of being stuck on some idyllic beach by stormy weather. But once on Highland Beach there was a cold front, combined with a series of flubs on my part, that threw me into an extended state of panic.

I hadn't checked my rain tarp before I launched, and it turned out that it was no longer waterproof. My VHF emergency radio was no longer working, and the backup VHF that I *always* bring was on the dash of the van back in Flamingo. My sail reefs with zippers, and the zipper was broken so I couldn't make my sail small enough to be safe in big winds. I had neglected to restock my water at the turnaround point in Everglades City since I thought, "Hey, I only used half of it on the way up. I'll be fine on the way back. If I don't get marooned." So, here I am marooned. Short on supplies. Critical gear not working. Ulp.

The weather folks later reported that the cold front that came through that time was "the strongest cold front to hit the area in five years." It didn't bring rain, but it did bring cold—lows in the thirties—and many days of fierce winds that blew the water away from Highland Beach and left me high and dry, with what looked like miles of deep, gooey muck to traverse before I could get to navigable water. It took me three days to crab-walk my boat out through the muck to water deep enough to sail on.

I made it back to Flamingo after a two-day sail with half a gallon of water and a couple of packs of raisins to spare. The crazy thing about this whole experience was—me. I became frantic to get out of there, to get off Highland Beach. For the first two days, the wind was blowing thirty knots, and the minute the sun went down the temperature plummeted. And yet, I would have launched if I could have gotten to the water. At night, when the wind backed off a bit, the water did come up to the shore. I could have sailed away. But sailing at night with temperatures in the thirties, a still-mighty wind, a sail that can't be shortened, no emergency radio. . . .

Sea purslane prairie. Photograph by Anne McCrary Sullivan.

I actually came real close to writing *the* note to my daughter, the one that says, "I'm really sorry I foolishly drowned myself in the Gulf of Mexico, but I always loved you and I always will." I found myself wondering, so, do you attach the note to the body or the boat? I could recognize that I was not thinking clearly, but I couldn't get control of my compulsion to get out of there, even if it meant launching at night. I was crazy. So I invented Safety Officer Ann to keep Crazy Sailor Ann from doing something really stupid. No matter what the water did, no matter how enticing it looked, Safety Officer Ann would not permit me to launch after 2:00 p.m. because she knew that I would not be able to reach any kind of shelter from the wind and cold if I launched later. She did her job well, and I was just together enough to make myself obey her.

That trip brought out things in me that I didn't know were there. Disorientation, bad decision-making, panic. The strength to slog through mud for hours at a time. And that something inside me that was determined to keep me safe, in spite of myself.

I did my very first long trek because of Valentine's Day, the most horrible of holidays. I hate it because it's this totally fake holiday when everybody is supposed to be all lovey-dovey to each other *if* they happen to be with somebody. And worse yet, people give each other chocolate—chocolate! *If* they're couples. I'd had a whole spate of chocolateless Valentine's Days. February was approaching, and I'd had it. I decided that during this particular February 14, I was going to go do something powerful. I set out into the Everglades on my own.

And that is why I continue to go out there. I've got this kind of imaginary balance sheet inside me and things just fly onto the negative side and stick. And I internalize them and that becomes my view of myself. Positives, they don't stick. People can be giving me promotions or As on tests or whatever and it doesn't go inside, doesn't make a change in how I feel about myself. I'm the only one who can do that. When I go out into the wilderness for a month and come back alive, I can always say, "*I did that*." And no matter how I may feel when I'm onshore, if I get to feeling emotionally puny or unloved or whatever during the rest of the year, even I can't deny that *I did that*. And that stays on the positive side of the balance sheet, and that's why I do it.

I'm one of those people who are recharged by solitude. Other people are recharged by people. In times of trouble, they say, "Can I come over?" I say, "Sorry, gotta go, see you later." For me, solo travel is a renewal. Sort of an annual tune-up. And another big reason is that I want to come back and say, "I did it," not, "We did it." Every decision, good or bad, was mine. If something breaks, I have to figure out what to do about that. It's empowering and exhilarating and humbling to make judgment mistakes and figure out how to get out of scrapes. There's some pride involved, for sure. But the bottom line is, I need to know how much strength there is in me, and how much courage. The only way to know that is to put myself to the test and find out.

There's this thing that happens to me on my treks, starting 'round about day three. When I leave the dock on the first day, I find I haven't really and truly left. I push off from shore and I'm immersed in my favorite sensations—wind on my face and water under my boat—and yet, I'm still thinking about emails, should-a-dones, and why did I say that thoughtless thing? I read, not to enjoy reading, but to keep my mind busy. But after three or so days, something shifts. The way I think of it is, "The book comes down." I lose the obsession to busy my mind. I'm there where I want to be, fully present. I step into a different way of perceiving what's around me. I'm likely to find myself just sitting. Breeze on my face. Warmth of the sand under my feet. Waves skittering up the shore. Joyful.

Ann Rougle's view: sunset and bugs.
Photograph by Ann Rougle.

So one year, after four days alone on the wild beaches of Cape Sable, after the book had come down and my senses had finally engaged with the marvels around me, I'm sailing up to Graveyard Creek. It's a perfect sailing day, and I am pristine and new and fresh and giddy with the joys of solitude in the wilderness. As I approach the camping area, I see three motorboats there. And guys. Cases of beer. Boombox blaring. And—I couldn't do it. I just couldn't. I knew I wouldn't be able to maintain my new state of being in that environment. So I turned right and sailed into the Shark River, into the mangrove estuary, into the interior. The wind was nudging me along. The current was giving me a free ride. Solitude was calling me. Never mind that I had no place to camp. I'd figure it out.

Mud. In these tidal mangrove Everglades, mud is part of the ever-changing landscape. Mud can extend for hundreds of yards from a Gulf beach at low tide, and in many areas it can be several feet deep. Muds vary in color and texture, from gray, clay-like calciferous marl to dark, silky organic "muck." Photograph by Holly Genzen.

GETTING STRANDED HERE ISN'T A BAD THING

Tom Buttle

KAYAKER AND PARK VOLUNTEER

I'm from Canada. While I'm down here, I volunteer in the park, killing exotics, mainly plants but the odd python, and try to get in two or three kayak trips 'cause I love it out on the Wilderness Waterway.

I bought my first canoe when I was thirteen, from paper route money. Being immigrants, my parents, by the time I hit thirteen, considered me to be an adult. They would drop me off at Algonquin Park for a month at a time by myself. I learned to live in the wild. I loved it. I had my own little pup tents, and after I got out of engineering, I improved them, made a high-tech pup tent. That was the tent I brought down in '72. My first wife and I used it on the chickees and beaches, the ideal first trip, when I did not know what a no-see-um was and never saw one on the entire trip.

We came down here and camped two nights at Flamingo for Christmas. Raccoons got our Christmas dinner. They had fun. Then we paddled from Flamingo to Everglades City. We bought maps and headed out the Buttonwood Canal, paddled up on the east side of Whitewater Bay, through Hells Bay to Lane Bay, got as far as the Shark River. The weather was ideal. There was hardly any wind, no big waves anywhere, so it really was a honeymoon trip.

I'd never seen mangroves before, never seen so many birds before, and the egrets and birds like that just amazed me. I've always loved birds, but you just don't see these birds up north. We do have white pelicans up there. They summer in northern Ontario.

I had to work a long time after that trip and then my wife died. Later, when my significant other came down with ALS, I retired, and we just traveled. When she died, I decided it would be nice to keep traveling. Traveling was my way of grieving. I bought a motorcycle, a 650 single cylinder, and rigged it up with panniers. To break it in, I rode down from Ontario and wintered in the Everglades. The next year when I came down, I met Cindy. She was working here as a seasonal ranger.

She said I should get something that would put me on the water. I had never kayaked before. So I went and bought a beater kayak for $350. A mistake, 'cause I didn't know anything about kayaks. It

had an ocean cockpit, which meant you could get in it on land, but if you ever tipped this, you'd never get back in it. I could get in by putting a paddle behind me and getting in on land. Hilarious, learning to get in and out of it gracefully.

I launched it first at Nine Mile Pond and promptly dumped it. I got slowly better, started feeling a little more comfortable, although it was very tippy. Then, to christen it, Cindy and I went out to camp on the chickees. But I couldn't get up on a chickee. Basically, I had to fall out of the kayak into the water to unload. With a larger cockpit you can use the ladder to get out without very much fuss at all. Canoe is even easier.

I named that first kayak *Erik* because it had a red top. It was fiberglass, and it carried a fair number of provisions. I got used to it, and I felt comfortable enough then to do the outside. Cindy dropped me off at Everglades City.

One of the things I love, being out there, is it is still wilderness. There's very little of that now unless you go north in Canada. Or Alaska. Even Alaska has a lot of people in it. I love wilderness, and this was a kind of wilderness I had never seen before.

The amount of dew down here is unreal. There's enough dew to keep raccoons alive on the keys. I still remember on the ground sites the first trip, the number of raccoons was just awesome. I assume it's the amount of water they get that controls the population. Back then, there were no pythons, so it really was what I would call a stable level of raccoons for the amount of water they could get.

So my first real trip in this kayak was from Everglades City down to Flamingo, and I started at the very north of the park, Picnic Key. It was a great spot. And from there, went down a couple more keys. At Hog Key. I actually found a pig's paw print on the beach. I thought that was cool. Then I had a long paddle to Highland Beach. I remember hitting Highland Beach pretty close to high tide, no big deal. In this kayak, you just take a run at the beach and then squirm out of the kayak, grab it, and pull it up before the next wave. I camped there with the "wild" coconut palms. It was beautiful.

That night I was camped within 15 feet of the water. I woke up the next morning, and "Where's the water?" It was 150 to 200 yards from shore. I'd never lived near oceans, and tides were new to me. So I carried all my gear and the kayak across the mudflat, loaded up in water two inches deep.

A couple of days later I had to cross Ponce de Leon Bay. I didn't realize it at the time, but about five rivers drain into Ponce de Leon Bay. At the tide change, when it's either sucking water in or pushing water out, it generates its own waves. I was paddling against the wind and the waves were crashing in. When I finally got to Cape Sable, I just aimed at it, went in like a rocket, and bailed out.

I was actually supposed to get to Middle Sable, but I thought I would stop on North Sable just so I could have some water, a whizz. I hadn't learned that in kayaks you need to take along something like a Gatorade bottle so you can relieve yourself. Anyway, I landed, and the waves were probably three to four feet high coming in. I swamped my kayak and had to pull it up on shore, roll it over, get water out of the cockpit so I could pull it farther up. Then I had a nice lunch and thought, well, I'll push off and go to Middle Sable.

To launch, I had to get in and try to put my spray skirt on before getting flooded and knocked over by waves. I tried ten or eleven times to launch. I failed miserably. I was basically marooned on North Sable.

The next day it calmed down a little, but I failed again two times to launch, and then I thought, well, maybe if I walk down North Sable a little farther, it does sort of circle. So I walked through water, towing my kayak with all my provisions, and got down to a point where I could finally launch. I felt like an idiot.

I was so tired I thought I'd better stay close to the shore. So I'm paddling along within a stone's throw of shore, and I get sucked into Lake Ingraham with the tide. It was unreal. I never got to the other Sable beaches. My speed was probably about three times what I could paddle because it's such an amount of water pushing into Lake Ingraham. I got out the other side into Florida Bay, and lo and behold, I had some wind behind me. So all of a sudden from being a day behind, I ended up right on my mark. Maybe it's the Buttle luck or something.

I enjoyed every minute of that trip except for getting stranded. Although getting stranded here isn't a bad thing. After failing to relaunch, I accepted being stranded. The weather was sunny, and the beach was gorgeous. I got to read for an extra half-day without fighting big waves. That beach is mainly finely crushed shells, and it glitters in the sun. High tides are marked by an interesting debris of seaweed, sponges, shells. The upper beach has hunter spiders and creeping vine-like plants before the grass and then small bushes and trees. I kept my back to the wind and listened to the roar of four foot waves. And because there was wind, there were very few no-see-ums or mosquitoes. Being stranded wasn't bad.

I love the Everglades because it is so different from what I've grown up with. The trees are different, the animals and reptiles are different. I love reptiles, by the way. I collected snakes when I was a kid, always let them go in plenty of time so they could find their winter homes. It still hurts me when I see dead snakes in the road. I tend to stop and toss them off into the bushes. It feeds the vultures.

Up north if you sit still, you'll see something happen maybe every two or three minutes. In the Everglades, if you sit down, you'll see something new every five or ten seconds, whether it's an anole moving along or . . . you know, there's so much life and movement in the Everglades. If you like life, it's down here in spades.

Red mangroves are an amazing tree, living in salt water the way they do. There are only a few trees in the world that can live in salt water. And the little pods that the mangroves make to re-create themselves. And those roots that go out in many directions into the mud.

I think of the people that lived out there before this became a park, and in my mind, they were tougher than most other pioneers. The number of pioneers was huge for what I would call a hostile environment. But I guess you do have plenty of fish.

Wilderness in general I love because, even as a ten- or eleven-year-old, it has always given me an inner peace. There is no such thing as stress when I am in the wilderness. Even when the wind is in my face, yeah, like I mumble at it and stuff like that, but I live with it. But if the wind's blowing and I'm at my destination, then I can just turn my back to the wind and read a book. I still want to be down here sometime and experience a hurricane. People think I'm crazy, but I've never seen a hurricane.

Mangrove with storm cloud.
Photograph by Anne McCrary
Sullivan.

Moving water tends to keep channels clear. A lot depends on how fast the water is moving. A tidal channel will stay open because the amount of water that is moved by the tides is mind-boggling. Ponce de Leon Bay just boggles my mind every time I paddle that area, thinking of the amount of water that moves there. When the tide's coming in, it's holding back all of the rivers, so the rivers back up. And then when the tide turns, the river water that was being held back, all of a sudden, starts flowing the other way. It's a huge amount of water. I respect the tides more now than I used to. The moon does a great job up there.

Cape Sable sponge. Photograph by Anne McCrary Sullivan.

And another thing, if water flows then you can pretty much always get out. The people that found all of these creeks probably just watched water flowing to get where they want to go. So if you're lost and you start to panic, you can actually stop, and if you know this sort of tide movement, you can always get unstuck. I have been lost, but I guess I've been a person that never panics anyway. That tends to be helpful, not only in the middle of nowhere.

So, yeah, you may get lost for a little while, the mangroves are easy to get lost in. But the only time I ever turn on my GPS is when I'm getting close to a destination that I've never been to before. I let it point me in the right direction when I am within a half kilometer, to sort of nail it down. There have been times, though, when I've kicked myself for not using my GPS. I got lost once, went from Hells Bay through the little creek into Lane Bay, no problem. On the return trip, I couldn't find that creek. I went back towards the chickee again, mentally looked at my map, had that direction. I tried it three times, could not find this creek again. I had to go all the way down Lane River, across Whitewater Bay, and back up into Hells Bay that way. So my stupidity forced me to go another fifteen miles. It would have cost me less than a minute to turn my GPS on and mark that spot, which I did on the subsequent trip.

But chart and compass just seem to be, for me, a more fun way. I guess, to me, wilderness does not have electronics involved. I feel more in the wilderness if I'm not pulling out some electronic device. And somebody found their way here a long time ago, just by following water flow, one way or the other. You can do it again. It's not that difficult. And the route they've picked for the Waterway isn't the only one. There's tons of little creeks that will get you from here to there. There's always in the Everglades more than one way to get there.

Even before those early experiences camping on my own in Canada, I was learning independence. I was born in London, and I was allowed to take buses and subway by myself from age six or seven to museums and galleries around the city. I spent a month every year at Mom's parents' farm picking mushrooms for breakfast, collecting sheep hair from barbed wire fence, biking to town for supplies. In school, skipping a couple of grades tended to make me an outcast so I learned to live by myself using books, and the great outdoors gave me peace.

Wilderness equals peace and tranquility for me. Sitting, hiking, paddling, watching nature pass by is just a thrill. The national parks and Crown lands are worth their weight in gold, and I hope I passed on some of this thrill to my kids by camping with them as they grew up. Myself, I am a fatalist, after outliving two women, and since I love solving problems and continuing to learn about our world, I expect to continue my travels in the wilderness until, eventually, I am scattered around the places I love.

Young fish and shellfish find protection in an intricate world beneath the surface. Photograph by JohnBob Carlos.

PART IV

THEY KNEW THESE MANGROVES WAY BACK WHEN

Horseshoe crabs (Limulus polyphemus), *Highland Beach. In spring and fall, especially at full and new moons, horseshoe crabs mate in large numbers on Gulf beaches. An extract found only in Limulus blood is used in testing vaccines. Photograph by Holly Genzen.*

STILL HERE: THE MAN AND THE MANGROVES

Oron "Sonny" Bass

WILDLIFE BIOLOGIST, EVERGLADES NATIONAL PARK

There's a spot around West Lake where there are a lot of little lakes surrounded by mangroves and buttonwoods, right where the grass comes in, kind of a transition zone. When we were kids, that was a great fishing area. The trail's right off the old road, so you muck through the sawgrass, and then into the mangroves and buttonwoods, and you're mucking around in that sulfurous mud and . . . you learn, at an early age, you get those odors in your soul. Everybody says, "Oh, god, isn't that smell awful!" And I go, "I don't know, it's kind of like heaven to me."

We used to go in there all the time, pulling boats, carrying motors. When I first started working in the park, I went in there with Bill Robertson and started doing the eagle counts. The more time you spend out there, the more you realize that you don't know about it, so the more time you want to spend in it. Nowhere else in the Park Service or anywhere in North America is there a force like that mangrove wilderness. We've had researchers from all over the world come to look at these mangroves, and one of the reasons is that it's still intact. It's been disturbed, no doubt. But it hasn't been destroyed.

My family moved here right after I was born, so this is the only home I've ever known, except for when I was in college. Other than that, I've never not been here. And I've known what I wanted to do since I was nine. As a child, I went out with Dad, uncles, family members, by myself, with other friends, in little boats with small motors. We'd go in the mangroves to fish.

I think some people are fortunate in always realizing what you wanted to be or do. I always wanted to be outdoors. Obviously, at nine years old I didn't know what it would take to do that. I'd ride down the roads, see a flagman, and think, "Well, he's outdoors. That'd be fun." Dad says, "You can't earn a living doing that." But I was raised with people that fished, raised with people that went in the woods all the time, so it was a part of me and I loved it.

Before I'd go to school in the morning, I'd go off and do something else. I'd come home from school and go into the woods. I spent time wandering around looking at things. I still do that. It's not something I was trained to do. It's something I was exposed to. It's like painters, you know, that aren't trained artists. Whether it's early in life or later in life, you pick it up. It's just what you do.

I majored in biology. Took every biology—invertebrate, herpetology, ichthyology, mammalogy, ornithology, general ecology, paleo vertebrate. I took plant ecology, plant taxonomy. I especially wanted to take what would get me in the field doing things. Took every field course I could find.

When I came back to Florida, I went to work for the National Audubon Society research lab down in the Keys. My interest in birds was really taking off. Then I met Bill Robertson and then Sandy Sprunt, head of the research center down here. He says, "I think I might have some part-time work for you."

So I went to work doing mostly bibliographical searches, but I would go in the field too. I would sit there at lunch time and read, and I would ask Sandy questions about this, about that. One day he says, "Go back to school." I thought, "Well, I've been thinking about it anyway." Bill said, "When you get through, come down and see me." So that was the beginning of my career here.

All the stars aligned at the right time. Nat Reed, undersecretary of the interior and a big supporter of the Everglades, had this vision of establishing research centers in national parks. Three parks were selected: Everglades, Yellowstone, and Redwoods. Gary Hendrix, our director at the time, hired me. My initial job was to be his assistant, to get the research program going.

Talk about spending time in the field! I went everywhere, places I had seen as a kid and more places too. It was so much fun, an incredible learning experience. Every day, something new. I was twenty-seven, maybe twenty-eight. It was a dream come true. I'm still a kid. Still a kid. But that's another story.

We had enough money in the park budget then to do a lot of things. A lot was expected of us too. Gary Hendrix had a lot of ethics behind his decision-making. It was rigorous. As it should be. It was a good research environment. One of the reasons these research sites started was that the National Park Service, through the Leopold Report in '94, had been criticized for not using good science in the management of the park. We've made huge gains in that realm. The Park Service has matured.

I have a lot of Highwaymen art. In 1975 or '76, my wife and I were at an art show, and the Buckner Brothers, Ellison and George, were there, and they're Highwaymen. This was before they became famous like they are now, but I knew some of their art. Nobody called them "Highwaymen." They just drew Old Florida landscapes.

Dolphins head to tail. Photograph by Anne McCrary Sullivan.

I'm walking through and I see this painting, and I stop. It's a Paurotis palm hammock with water, and it's in a rainstorm. I said, "I've been there!" So I talked to Ellis. He says, "The lowest I'd go is five hundred dollars." Well, that was a lot of money. My wife and I talked and talked about it. And I bought it. It's like she was telling this guy the other night, "We didn't even have a field crate to sit on, but we had that painting hung on the wall." It's just one of those things, you know, you're struck by it because it's part of you.

We used to fish in places like around the Shark River, before those really big mangroves came down . . . spectacular. I hear people say, "Nobody will ever see that again." Not in our generation. But the one thing about that forest, it's resilient. This is not the first time it's been wiped out by a storm. And it will not be the last. But to see it at its apex . . . amazing.

When I'm flying, doing surveys on eagles, looking down, and I see this eagle nest on top of one of those tall mangroves, I think, "Wow! That bird's got a penthouse! A great forest to look at, and talk about ocean view." There's nothing wrong with words like *primeval, primitive, pristine* blah blah, but it isn't that. It's seeing a view that makes you part of it. It's a part of you. It's part of me. It is. You're flying over looking at this, and then you're down on the ground in the middle of it.

People say it does things to you. Yeah, it feeds your soul. Makes you feel connected. It's like an artist being connected to a piano or to a brush in their hand. Or a composer or a singer or a dancer. They do it because they love it. They'd do it for nothing. They do it because they have to. It's part of who you are and what you are and so you just do it. And it's like that for me in the mangroves.

The aerial surveys are still going on. Bill Robertson started the eagle one in '59, and we continue today, monitoring the eagle nests, looking at nest production and activity. Bill and Sandy went and found them in '59 and in the sixties when they were in trouble because of DDT. Audubon was one of the ones that started it, along with Bill with the Park Service, because this ecosystem had one of the largest contiguous populations left. You could still see eagles like they used to occur. It was important to get that documented and to see how they were doing. Only through long-term work can you know what you've got and protect it. Bill Robertson had incredible foresight.

He was a very deliberate person. You'd ask him a question, and he'd think about it a long time before he'd answer. Unless it was something that really agitated him. I'll never forget him sitting in meetings, with his hands to his head, and if something was being said that just really aggravated him, he'd shake his head. You'd hear him over there kind of mumbling to himself. Then he'd throw his hand up, and he'd stand up and look at the floor: "Well, you know, I'm not sure." He was very polite. He was going to disagree in a way that didn't offend anybody. He was just pointing out something. "You know, you need to be looking at it from a little different perspective."

Bill's undergraduate major was English. In his dissertation, he said something very profound. He said, "The Everglades were half destroyed before they were half understood." In other words, things were so altered before we started paying attention that it's hard for us to understand how this thing worked prior to that. It took me a long time to come to that realization.

So while we can all be positive about saving wading birds—none of us would be opposed to that—there's a larger matter of trying to understand how they fit in the system. Because it's not a static system. Things are going to change. What you want to do is, you want to keep those changes as natural as possible and maintain the productivity of its unaltered state.

Restoration implies that you restore. You do. But what you're restoring is the functionality of it. You're not restoring it to exactly what it was because you can't do that.

Right now, the biggest threat to the mangrove forests is sea level rise. You can go look at the erosion that's taking place out there. It's happening at an alarming rate, all the way up the west coast of the park. Especially, most pronounced, you can see it at the Capes, in those forests up around Big Sable, Little Sable, and further up. The confounding thing that goes along with sea level rise is the dynamic wave action you get. So the beaches on Cape Sable are much smaller than they were. They're washing away. Things are changing, and they're changing rapidly.

Highland Beach has changed dramatically. And of course, some of it's natural. Hurricanes have done a lot. Andrew came across the state and exited right there at Highland Beach. It just leveled all those mangroves. Not a mangrove standing. And then, there's the tidal surge. As the storm goes out, it sucks out water, then it blows it all in again. And then it goes back out again. All that action cuts channels through the beach.

We did aerial surveys right after Hurricane Andrew. You've got all the fresh water coming down, the nutrient flow coming in, all the black-looking tannin in the water from all those mangrove trees. You fly over it, and all that stuff is being released, and you smell the methane in the air, and I can't help but think how incredibly fertile it is. So a few years later, here are all these young mangrove trees out there. As you watch them over time, they get bigger and bigger, and you're watching it unfold right in front of you, watching the whole process. These things that take a long time. Studies are usually only funded for a very short period. One of the great things about Bill was that he was able to do the long-term studies. Now, all the programs that I work

The Nightmare. This narrow, root-filled channel provides a link through the mangroves that allows one to paddle from Everglades City to Flamingo without going into the Gulf. It can only be traversed at high tide. Photograph by Holly Genzen.

January mangrove-scape.
Photograph by Holly Genzen.

on are at least twenty-five years ongoing. It is remarkable. You can look at this over a period of time, and you can see the shifts that take place.

One of the things Bill always regretted was that there was no bird book on the park. So we got together before his death, and we started one. So of late, I've gotten an

illustrator, and he's a very gifted writer too, and we're working on a bird book for the park. I hope it comes to fruition. This is birds, not *of* the Everglades, birds *in* the Everglades. So we want the mangroves there, and we want the birds that are associated with the mangroves. And that way, people can come in here and, I hope, be connected to it, by not only seeing the birds but seeing the trees they're in and knowing why they're unique.

I was watching a Highwayman. He was sitting there, and I was watching him, and I could see that what he was painting was in his mind, and he knew exactly what he was doing. He puts the bird over here, he's got the trees and the reflection, and he's got this orange sunset. I'm watching him, thinking, yeah, he's seen this so many times, he knows exactly what it is. He doesn't need a picture in front of him. I'm envious of people like that. No, it's not envy. It's awe. It's awe. It's like, wow. How do you *do* that? Well, I tend to ramble sometimes. I can tell you right now, you'd have to pry the words out of Bill Robertson.

It is remote. It is hard to work there. It does have bugs. That tends to drive a lot of people away. But the mangroves are an important area. Any excuse I can find, I always want to go out there. And when I'm there, I watch the tide, what it brings in. I've seen manta rays jump, eagle rays—tarpon by the hundreds. Some mornings in Tarpon Bay—tarpon busting, mullet jumping all over the place—schools of dolphin. It's a phenomenal place. I don't know how you describe something like that. It's one of those things, you gotta see it. I can't tell you about it. You gotta be there. Then you'll understand.

Florida Bay. Photograph by Ann Rougle.

SERIOUS, SERIOUS BACKCOUNTRY

Leon Howell

SEASONAL INTERPRETIVE RANGER, EVERGLADES NATIONAL PARK

When I think of that mangrove wilderness, I think of how it looks when you come around Northwest Cape and all of a sudden the beaches end, and as far as you can see is mangrove forest. There's lots of living and dying going on there, everything from microbes to large animals. It's an area unique in this country and certainly to some degree in the world. And the tall, well-developed, deep dark mysterious area at the Shark River is just spectacular, breathtaking.

There's history there. People lived there. People tried to farm on the Cape—coconut plantation, cattle. People were apparently buried at Graveyard Creek. I think of Ed Watson, "Bloody Ed," and all those early pioneer people. Then there's the prehistory. You find broken pieces of pottery all along Cape Sable. At Canepatch and Camp Lonesome, you're camping on old middens. It's impossible for me not to think of those that were here before me, the voices, the discussions of the day's issues. The mangrove forest is not only alive with plants and animals, but with rich human history as well.

When I was a kid in South Miami, fishing took me in the mangroves. And I liked plants, I liked crayfish, I liked rocks. So . . . fishing has always been to me, in addition to the fun, a way of *being in the place*. And there was no place better than the Everglades, *this* place, of all the places I've been, in regard to its science and nature. And its fishing.

I was away from South Florida for twenty-four years, in the Coast Guard. When I came back in '85 as a grown up, I was all over this place fishing, and with a much more evolved interest in science and nature.

Michael Grunwald in his book, *The Swamp,* wrote that if the Grand Canyon is a breathtaking painting, then the Everglades is a complex drama where everything has a role. The first actor on the stage in Grunwald's drama was geology.

A lot of people glaze over when you talk about geology. I don't know why because it just tickles me to death. To understand the Everglades, including its mangroves, you have to come to grips with geology. First off, it's not totally flat out there; if it was, it wouldn't look like it does. The rock of South Florida dips slowly to the south and west, becomes close to sea level. Way back, five thousand years ago, when sea levels were twenty feet lower, there wasn't much sediment on that rock. As the sea level came up, sediments built up a substrate and set the condition for mangroves.

Geology, changing sea levels, the placement of the rock, the modern climate, all are related to the mangrove forest in one way or another, particularly our deepest mangrove forests up around Shark River.

I think the Gulf Coast is extraordinary—from Harney River south to Northwest Cape, that complex of creeks and those bays that are very different at low tide than high tide. You get back in there early in the morning, it's like the dawn of time.

And in Florida Bay, where it's dotted with mangrove islands, particularly early, when it's glass calm and there's a little mist in the air, you can't differentiate the horizon, can't tell the water from the sky, and you have these islands out there that seem to be floating just above the surface of the water (see photo on page 160). It's a pretty odd sensation, a really cool thing, those islands just sort of floating. It's a bit disorienting, really.

I've never been much of a camper, but when I got back down here, I says I gotta go on the Wilderness Waterway, gotta get out there. I did two ten-day trips with a buddy. He had a canoe, I had a canoe, six hundred pounds of gear each, we were not freeze-dried backpackers. We had little motors that would allow us to cover twenty-five miles in a day if we wanted to.

One year we launched from Chokoloskee and came down to Camp Lonesome. We used chickees going and coming, but we'd set up on ground sites for three or four days and explore with canoes, fish, take pictures, always had cameras.

I'd never done any serious backcountry camping like that, no radios, no nothing. And . . . something I didn't expect happened. You know, I've heard talk about a "wilderness experience." I'm not sure what a "wilderness experience" is, but when I was out there, there was a shift in my perception and in my emotions that was so subtle I didn't notice it until I returned.

When I came back, both times this happened, first time I thought, "No, that's an anomaly." But it happened a second time. You get back to the boat ramp, and there's

Limestone, Buttonwood Canal. The bedrock of the Everglades is limestone, a porous sedimentary rock composed of numerous layers of sand, calcium carbonate, and the shells of small marine invertebrates. Photograph by Holly Genzen.

the car and there's an airplane, and somebody's got a radio on—it's all incongruous. It's startling. You know, I thought, I was out there, I didn't have a whole lot to do but I wasn't bored. I got up early, went to sleep well (at least, after the first couple of nights). I thought, "Well, damn. Maybe that's a wilderness experience."

So I don't know what that is you get out there, but it's an experience, a personal, internal experience that I would have never had in my life if I hadn't done something like that. I would have no clue about it, and now I have at least an idea of what, to me, is a wilderness experience. Something happened to me out there. I didn't know it was happening until I came back.

More recently, I've done some camping trips out there, three or four nights, taking motorboats with canoes on top, stay at Camp Lonesome or Canepatch or Willy Willy, fish with my buddies and drink whiskey at night. I didn't get the same effect. It wasn't long enough. I think you have to be out there a while. And I might have brought too much with me from civilization. I mean, it was fun, it was great, and I went into places that were serious, serious backcountry, but I wasn't startled by a car radio when I came back.

I was camping at Graveyard Creek, and my buddy went up to Harney River to see if he could catch dinner. I says I'm gonna go as far up Graveyard Creek as I can. Sunrise. I got way back up the creek until it was canopied over and very narrow but deep. I couldn't see around the bend, and you know, there's nobody around, and I hear this commotion in the water ahead of me. I couldn't see it. It was up the creek a ways . . .

Mangrove-sawgrass ecotone.
Photograph by Anne McCrary
Sullivan.

whoosh! And then within seconds I heard it again, closer. Now the hackles on the back of my neck are standing up. All of a sudden my canoe started rocking.

It was dolphins! They were coming down the creek at a good clip, and I could not turn my canoe around in that narrow creek. Water was five or six feet deep, but . . . wow, what are they doing up here? Then I realized they're up here looking for things to eat, and it's probably routine. Since then, I've seen that a lot of times.

Another time I was in a canoe between Lake Ingraham and the beaches. There's a complex of shallow bays back in there, and on a low tide it looks like Saudi Arabia. It's just exposed mud except for these little tidal runoffs—great because the birds are right along the creek banks foraging in the mud, and if there's any fish at all, they will be in that runoff.

So I'm pushing up one of these little streams. There were redfish in there, chasing the little crabs and the bait fish, and there were sharks six and seven feet long. They could not even get their dorsal fins submerged in this tidal runoff. They were in that shallow, narrowly confined water for the same reason that we were all there—for the life that was there. They were eating it. I was looking at it, trying to catch it. I thought, wow, who'd have thought of a six-foot shark in eighteen inches of water in a creek that's only eight feet wide? And they know their way in, know their way out, and know when to come. Look at all this stuff it's got to eat! Shark sense.

After that, any time I had a person with me at low tide, I would pole my boat up into those places, and people would be startled—sharks chasing the mullet, the mullet running, trying to get away, everything bumping the boat's hull. Didn't happen every time, of course, but every time it did . . . you know, your jaw just goes slack.

If you don't want to care about the mangrove forest, I can't make you, and I'm probably not going to lecture on why you should. There are a lot of people on the planet that for one reason or another are either just not fascinated by it or they've got bigger problems. You can't talk about the wonders of the mangrove forest with somebody who's trying to feed two kids and doesn't know where tomorrow's groceries are coming from. But for others, you can tie this wilderness, the South Florida overall ecosystem, to their daily lives, by water.

If water quality and quantity goes way down, then wells are not going to give water. You're not going to be able to take a shower, walk around on South Beach in a Speedo with that emerald earring and a designer beer. I'm sure that some people on the beach *are* aware of that. And I'm sure that plenty aren't.

I care about it. For those reasons, certainly, but it's really the experiences that this place gives me. It lets me fool around with science and nature. It lets me get away from things, to refuge. And I like it just 'cause it's there. I always have, and I always will. I care about it. And worry about it.

I see things as a big picture—the landscape. But I like to know what that little flower is too. Just for fun. Rick Seavey helped me a lot with plants, and I helped him with geology. We each had a period in our lives when that's what we did. I taught geology and he taught plants. He came over and helped me in my yard.

And I worked with him and Jean on some of their projects, removing exotics from the park, including Brazilian pepper on Cape Sable. When we were doing that, the early 2000s, I got to walk every inch of that beach, every inch of the prairies behind the beaches, every inch of the hammocks behind that, and into the black mangrove areas. I had been out there a million times in my boat, but when you pull a boat up on the beach out there, subject to wind and tide, you don't walk four miles away from it. Tony Terry, the ranger, would take us out, drop us off, we'd have all our equipment and some volunteers with us. We worked pretty hard for about four hours. Then we'd just fool around for the rest of the day. I was with Seavey, so if I had any plant questions, you know, there it was.

I was really fortunate to be hired as an intern ranger in 2005 by Alan Scott. I was fatigued with guide-fishing, didn't want to do that anymore. I had applied at the park a couple of times, and nothing happened. It's pretty competitive. Then, after Hurricane Wilma, maybe people didn't want to come back, so he got to the bottom of the barrel, pulled my application out, called me, like first of December. I mean, it was late. He says, "Leon, you don't put any references down." I says, "I haven't worked for anybody in twenty years!" And then I thought, "Do you know Rick and Jean Seavey?" So he called them, and then he called me back very quickly. I don't even think he offered me a job. He just said, "Can you be here day after tomorrow?"

Evening light Lane Bay. Photograph by Anne McCrary Sullivan.

I've realized that being a science and nature nut, being a fishing guide, getting out in the boat, it all was practicing for this job. I had a rebellious youth. I was a rabble rouser, problems with teachers and my parents. I grew up real quick 'cause I joined the service at seventeen, had a career as a military officer, then a fishing guide, then a park person. But I always considered myself sort of a hippie in disguise.

I'm still a little bit of a rebel these days, a person that questions authority. It's under control now, doesn't get me in trouble, at least not too much. I've survived. Not all of my buddies survived. If it wasn't Vietnam, it was drugs or going to jail. I was the kind of guy who went right to the edge but didn't step over.

Even when I was my angriest and most rebellious, I was reading George Gamow's *A Star Called the Sun* and *A Planet Called Earth*. Even then, at fourteen, fifteen, sixteen years old. So. I is what I is. I've been very lucky, I think, when I look back. Certainly fortunate to be able to work for the park, do something that does not seem like work to me. I look forward to going to work and the hustle-bustle, the conversations. I look forward to the visitors. All in all, I can't believe I get paid to do this. It should almost be against the law, it's so cool.

My fishing partner, Cass Sumrall, is not so much interested in the science and nature, but he is interested in deep backcountry, so we'd go up the river, take a creek, and break out of the mangroves, into freshwater prairie. We loved exercising the navigation skills it took to get in and out of these places, pre-GPS. We would do that for days. A lot of fish. A lot of wilderness. A lot of cool plants. I would look at the plants as much as I would look at the fish.

One day I was with Cass in the backcountry north of Flamingo, and he was standing on the bow fishing. He turns around and I've got my little magnifier, looking at some vegetation. I was interested in the aquatic stuff up in those areas. With a lot of rain, you get bladderwort up there, and when the rains stop, that bladderwort dies back 'cause it's real sensitive to salt water.

"Leon, what are you doing?"

"I'm looking at this plant here. I want to know what the hell it is."

He just shakes his head. But he's a great fishing partner. He likes being in the backcountry as much as anybody, just for different reasons. As far as my life as an angler goes, I have long since quit caring whether I caught fish or not.

A GUIDE TO THE
WILDERNESS WATERWAY
OF THE EVERGLADES
NATIONAL
PARK

WILLIAM G. TRUESDELL

MAPPING THE EVERGLADES MANGROVE WILDERNESS

William G. Truesdell

AUTHOR OF THE FIRST GUIDEBOOK TO THE
EVERGLADES WILDERNESS WATERWAY

August 1968: The Water Wilderness Boat Trail was completed during the month, and Superintendent Allin and Assistant Chief Ranger Stokes made an inspection run of the entire trail from Flamingo to Everglades City. District Naturalist Truesdell assisted personnel in placing 80 markers along the Trail from Everglades City to the Harney River. The District Naturalist drew strip maps of the entire waterway and is writing a text to accompany the maps in a handbook on the Mangrove Wilderness.

January 1969: District Naturalist Truesdell continued to work on the Guide to the Wilderness Waterway. . . . On January 29th, a trip through the waterway was made to check on the accuracy of the charts and to assign numbers to each marker.

February 1969: District Naturalist submitted final pages of text for the Guide to the Wilderness Waterway to the University of Miami Press. Strip maps were completed by a cartographer and reviewed and corrected by the District Naturalist. On night duty, the District Naturalist covered the mangrove country from Tarpon Bay to Cabbage Bay, Rocky Creek Bay, Lostman's Creek, and the Wilderness Waterway north to Everglades City. During the day, while on night duty, the District Naturalist started numbering the markers on the Wilderness Waterway.

March 1969: District Naturalist Truesdell spent several days and nights rewriting and correcting the text of the Guide to the Wilderness Waterway. Numbering of the channel markers on the Wilderness Waterway continued.

—Chief Park Naturalist Reports, Everglades National Park, 1968–1969

Visitors to Florida's Everglades National Park who want something more than the usual water and land tours now have a fully charted and marked 99-mile wilderness waterway from Flamingo to Everglades City. Officially open to small-boat navigation this year, the waterway winds through rivers, creeks, canals and bays in the mangrove area of the park

—The New York Times, February 19, 1970

FINDING BILL

Anne: Did I tell you how I found you finally? You were a mystery. We didn't know if you were alive or dead or a ghost, and I had googled you forever and couldn't find anything. Then, when I was in the park archives, trying to learn anything I could about the Waterway and its origins, I found the district ranger's monthly reports. In one of these, I read that in 1966 they were trying to recruit you from Shenandoah.

Bill: Who would try to do a thing like that? That's a nice story.

Anne: When I got to the reports that you wrote yourself, you were signing them "William Truesdell." Fine. That's your name. And then I come to a report where you sign "Bill Truesdell." I thought, I've never searched for a Bill Truesdell. I went back and googled again, "Bill Truesdell." Something came up about a volunteer named Bill Truesdell leading wildflower walks in Joshua Tree National Park. I knew it had to be you.

Kathy: He goes by Bill most of the time. His wife calls him William when she wants his attention.

Bill: We seldom use William anymore. I don't know him.

Anne: Well, he's still out there in the mangroves. That little guidebook you wrote has been out in many a boat, traveled many a mile. When Holly and I first started going out there, it was our lifeline, and that's been true for so many paddlers.

EARLY DAYS IN EVERGLADES NATIONAL PARK

Bob Kerr was the assistant chief ranger at Shenandoah when I was there. When he had transferred down to Everglades as the chief ranger, he said, "Hey, Bill, you might like this. There's an interpretive park ranger/naturalist position in Everglades." I said, "Sounds interesting. I'll go." I didn't even ask the family.

In 1967, I went to Homestead as a park naturalist, then in June 1968, I went to Everglades City as the district naturalist. Then the Park Service lumped interpretation and resource management into one program, which meant that there was no interpretive division, no resource management division, and no protection division. It was all one job and you got to do everything, which had its benefits. I have laughingly said I gave environmental study tours in the daytime and went on gator poaching patrols at night.

It was a popular thing to do waterway trails and guides, early seventies, I think. When it was first established, there were no limits or controls or rules for the

Art Johnson and Larry Dale install a marker for the new Wilderness Waterway. Photograph by William G. Truesdell.

Waterway marker 17, high tide, 1970. Photograph by William G. Truesdell.

Everglades Wilderness Waterway. We didn't have that many campsites, and we didn't have that many users. Canoe use wasn't big at that time. Kayaks? What are they? Never even heard of them.

Once we laid it out, the Waterway had to be marked, of course. We would go out there with a flat barge loaded with sixteen-foot posts, use a water pressure pump to dig them in. Here, Larry is in uniform, Art in work clothes coated with insect repellent (see photo on page 171). I took this photo in mid-August 1968. I tell you it was hot and buggy! We had a government issue repellent that had the same basic ingredients as commercial repellents but ten times the strength. You could stand one dousing, but when you put on another layer, it would start the skin burning. We sprayed our clothes and most often wore long sleeves.

Banding ospreys. 1968. John Ogden on Ladder, Bill Truesdell below. Photograph by Ogden and Truesdell.

SCIENCE IN THE MANGROVES

Bill: This marker almost sank out of sight every year during high tide (see photo on page 171). If it was an extreme high tide, you couldn't find the marker at all because it would be under water.

When the Waterway was first established and I was putting together the guidebook, we primarily had motorboaters in mind. There weren't many campsites along the way, they were spread pretty well, and the distances would challenge a canoeist.

There was a lot of scientific work going on in the mangroves.

This is John Ogden, banding ospreys on one of the small keys in Florida Bay (see photo on the left). John and I, and a couple of other people, including a lady by the name Johnnie Fisk, also banded birds down there. One year somebody invited Johnnie to come down and stay at the Lostmans patrol cabin. She stayed for two weeks banding birds, and she found all sorts of great things, including a Cuban warbler, which was an unusual species for the area.

Ernest Choate came down there too. Ernie wrote a guide to birds' names. If you want to find out who a bird was named for, LeConte's thrasher, for example, you can look in Ernie's book and he tells you who LeConte was, and if you want to know who a warbler was named for or Anna's hummingbird—Anna, duchess of Rivoli. Ernie collected all that knowledge and put it in *The Dictionary of American Bird Names*. He spent a week or so down there at Lostmans River patrol cabin. He was working on the book at the time, and he was just a dictionary himself. We'd be walking along, and we'd mention a bird, and he'd say, "Did you know it was named for so and so?" He had it all in his head.

The Lostmans Patrol Station was an old trailer right on the north edge of the river just before the exit. There is a huge sandbar at the entrance to the river, so when the tide was out, if it was real low, you couldn't get in.

I remember one day as we were coming in to Lostmans River, we stopped at the dock and said, "Uh-oh, let's not stay." We paddled back out to the middle of the river and wiped the sandflies off our arms and necks and faces. They can be as bad as mosquitoes. That patrol station was still operative when I left there in '70.

Kathy: We have a photo somewhere of Ogden being dive-bombed by an osprey who said, "No you won't touch my baby!" He would go out there with all of his paraphernalia wrapped around him, sort of like a soldier, a mercenary out there with all his bullets, except these are bird bands and all this equipment, and his ladder and his camera. He was just loaded down.

Bill: I believe John Ogden may have been the first full-time bird expert in the park, and there was not a lot of scientific information available then. So a lot was still out there to be documented. I remember very happily helping John and Bill Robertson with osprey banding, primarily on my off time, carrying ladders through the mangroves on keys in Florida Bay. There were eagle nests and osprey nests located pretty close together, and their interactions were great.

I was hooked on birds when I was down there. So I've got 4,330 pictures of birds. There was an island, somewhere around Lostmans River, that had a frigatebird colony on it, a nesting colony. That must have been '68, '69. It was fun to see.

I learned something the other day. We were on our vacation trip, and we stopped at a museum. They had a fossil relative of the frigatebirds, from ancient times, two million years old or so. It was pretty much the same size as contemporary frigatebirds, in rock slab at least three foot square. The bird took up the whole slab, the legs and the wing pattern showing.

MANGROVES FROM THE AIR

That's Ralph Miele with the plane (see photo below). The nice thing about being up in the air with Ralph was you could get something like this aerial shot (see photo on page 175). I think that might be the Harney River.

When I was assigned part time to the exotic plant removal program, I got in some fun flying time with Ralph. For about three months, I flew all over the park identifying and mapping populations of exotic species. I had been asked to do a survey of the casuarina, the invasive Australian pines along the coast. At Highland Beach, there was a huge stand of them, must have been forty or fifty right on the shore, and with beach erosion it was to the point where we were going to lose the turtles that were trying to nest there. We flew that whole area mapping casuarinas.

The other main portion of my job description at that time was law enforcement. I would make daily and nightly boat patrols for illegal alligator poachers and commercial stop-netting fishermen. I was trying to remember the name of the guy that we ran up on the beach one night, gator poaching. He was trying to get away from us and finally beached himself on Highland Beach, tried to drag the alligators out

Ralph Miele pulls the anchor line, 1969. Photograph by William G. Truesdell.

of the boat up into the trees. Of course, we could see the tracks. Then he was stuck on the beach. He had a pretty good boat that was confiscated along with everything else he had.

An area of the western mangroves as seen from the park plane flown by Ralph Miele. Photograph by William G. Truesdell.

SANDFLY ISLAND

Sandfly Island was one of my favorite sites around Everglades City. We created a one-mile trail out of what used to be a quarter-mile trail, and we started bringing in kids from Collier County, fourth, fifth, and sixth graders (see top photo on page 176). We established a National Environmental Study Area (NESA site).

We chose Sandfly Island as a nature trail site, and later it was designated a NESA site because it had early native cultural resources, including the remains of shell mounds. It had also been occupied by early settlers whose home and garden remains were still evident.

The old nature trail started at the dock, ran about a half mile toward the west, and ended at an old tamarind tree. It didn't get into the historic homestead site or offer a good example of the shell mound, which raised the elevation and made it "livable." We wanted to show examples of shell mounds so we could relate the story

Students participate in a clean–up project on Sandfly Island dock, 1970. Photograph by William G. Truesdell.

Johnny Galvin and Guy Michener constructing the Sandfly Island boardwalk, 1970. Photograph by William G. Truesdell.

of early native occupancy. So we constructed a trail that would make a complete loop around the island, through the homestead site and their vegetable garden (we were told that they grew tomatoes), then through the low-lying mangroves portion of the island. The biggest problem was that during high tides the trail would be under water. So we built a boardwalk. Everglades City maintenance supervisor Johnny Galvin, seasonal ranger Guy Michener, and I worked on that boardwalk (see bottom photo on page 176).

When we were able to open the trail, a local fourth-grade teacher, his first name was Roy, brought his class immediately. Roy helped me with environmental education classes and getting his and other schools involved. Sammy Hamilton, the boat tour concessioner at Everglades City, provided transportation for school classes to visit the Island.

SOME FAVORITE PLACES

Here's Darwin at Darwin's Place (see below). Darwin was a nice gentleman—friendly, sociable. He liked being out there (see photo on page 178).

Arthur Darwin, hermit, at his home on Possum Key, 1970. Photograph by William G. Truesdell.

Some of my favorite places out there are the higher elevated places like Johnson Mound, off the south side of Lostmans River. It was an archaeological site. There used to be palm trees on the mound, and it used to be walkable, so you could get back in there to the mound area, about half a mile. I remember it as being fairly easy to park a boat on the shore and just go on in. I would be curious to know if there are palm trees still there.

Hells Bay is another area I like a lot just because it's a fun place to get into. You can't just turn the corner and go straight in, you got to turn the corner, go right, go around, and turn back, and then you get in. It was called Hells Bay on all of the maps, and Gates of Hells Bay was right next door, south a little.

At Watson's Place, I'm remembering one beautiful red-flowered royal poinciana. That was a beautiful tree. He had kept the grass down in front of it recently enough that you could walk to it. I hear there's Brazilian pepper there now, lots of it. We bring the Marines to do exotics removal sometimes in Joshua Tree. Sounds like they need a group of volunteers to clean exotics at Watson's site.

Oh, and Deer Island Run! That used to be one of my favorites because it gave me an alternative to the usual. Instead of following the Waterway route, we would go around Deer Creek to Deer Island just for the hell of it. We called it the Deer Island

William G. Truesdell at Everglades City, circa 1970.

Run. It was a favorite snook fishing area for a few locals. There may be a lot of growth since then. It looks marshy on the map.

I remember at Plate Creek Bay there's a sandbar (or used to be), and going south, we would have to wait till the tide was right to get over that sandbar at the entrance to the bay. But the other thing was, if you looked across, you could see the tallest mangroves of Plate Creek Bay right at the entrance. That was helpful at night when you could just make out the tops of the trees.

Ranger Truesdell gives a guided boat tour to Kingston Key, 1968.

Kingston Key was one of the outside islands of the Ten Thousand Islands. We had a dock out there, and we used to take Sammy Hamilton's boats out (see photo on page 179). I would give guided walks for groups on Kingston Key. We offered daily or twice-daily tours out there in the winter season.

HURRICANES

Kathy: We evacuated once for a hurricane, but it didn't actually hit Everglades City. It was Hurricane Camille. Remember what Camille did to the Gulf Coast? We watched it go by. We said, "Oh my goodness, this is going to be a big one."

Bill: Not too many people talk about or remember Hurricane Donna and Hurricane Betsy. Donna came through in 1960, crossed Florida Bay and came in at Flamingo, washed mattresses and beds from the Flamingo lodge a mile into the Everglades. As it went up the coast, it trimmed eighty to one hundred-foot-tall mangroves of the west coast, around Shark River, down to forty or fifty feet. Betsy was in '65.

That was before we got there, of course. Researching for this Waterway guide, I read an awful lot. Some of these books, you couldn't put 'em down. I also read the monthly ranger reports. One ranger reported that a sailboat owner went up the Shark River as far as he could go because the hurricane was descending upon him. He tied his boat in spread-eagle spider webbing, the lines with enough flexibility to go up with the tide, and he said the wind gauge blew away at 165 miles an hour. Nobody talks about Donna, but it had some strength.

THE NIGHTMARE

Kathy: I haven't heard of the . . . what is it? The Terribles?

Anne: Oh, the Nightmare? The Nightmare is the interior passage, the link that made it possible to cut between Broad Creek and the Harney River. When this link was established, one could go all the way from Everglades City to Flamingo without entering the Gulf.

Bill: They now call that the Nightmare?

Anne: Yes. Maybe one of the first people through there got stuck. You can't get through on a low tide. Maybe it was a nightmare experience.

Bill (laughing): Nightmare is good. I like it.

Anne: How was that shown on the map in your guidebook?

Bill: I'm curious too. That's a good question [consults the map]. Let's see. This is your passageway. That's probably what you're calling the Nightmare. *Between marker 17 and 21 very shallow, between 21 and 23 passable only at high tide.*

Kathy: And you better know when high tide is.

Anne: Well, the Nightmare is there on all the official charts and maps now.

Bill: I approve. Good idea.

Kathy: These things have reasons. They describe what somebody needs to know.

AFTER FIFTY YEARS

Bill: About five years ago, we were at the Kiwanis International Convention in Miami, June or July. We were outside doing something, and here comes the rainstorm in the middle of the afternoon. I said, "Hey, we're in Florida!"

Kathy: I remember how in Everglades City you could set your clock by that afternoon rain between 4:30 and 5:00. In the rainy season. Every day.

Bill: After fifty years, what does one say? I would love to go back and see Everglades City.

Ralph Miele opens the seaplane door at an airstrip in the Park, 1967. Photograph by William G. Truesdell.

THE FLYING ALLIGATOR

Ralph Miele

RANGER PILOT, EVERGLADES NATIONAL PARK

Everybody had a nickname. I was "Miele Bug" or "The Flying Alligator." I learned to fly in 1939. They had a civilian pilot training program prior to World War II when Germany was just starting to move. I'd been sneaking around the airport, helping sweep the hangars, push airplanes around. I decided to get my private license and then went on for a commercial license and instructor ratings. So in the war, I was flying out in the Pacific, four-engine Douglas transports. Everything going west was fresh fish and cargo, and everything coming east was stretcher cases.

My first job in Everglades National Park was fire control aide. It was the '51–'52 fire season, and I was in the tower looking around to see if there's any smokes, any lightning strikes, or people setting fires around their camps. I knew absolutely nothing about the national park, but while I was up in that tower, about three months, I did a lot of reading about outdoorsmen in the Everglades in the late 1800s, early 1900s. I read about the original premises to establish the park. I got interested. And then the April rains came, and they took me down from the tower. You know, no fires.

For the winter '52–'53 season, they wanted me back as a dispatcher. Big promotion. As a fire control aide, I got ninety-seven cents an hour. They hired me back at ninety-eight cents an hour. That's forty cents more a week, which would buy four more loaves of bread. That lasted a few months. By then I had started flying for the park.

Whenever they had a fire, they'd hire airplanes, and I was flying them. So they made me the first ranger pilot for the entire National Park Service. Before I was a ranger pilot, they had no nomenclature for it. "What's a pilot? Is that a boat pilot?" Kind of funny.

And I got the Park Service's first airplane. One day I'm up in the office looking at a listing of surplus stuff. I saw there was this Super Cub out in Salt Lake City. George Fry, chief ranger, was in the office. I said, "There's a Super Cub available with the Interior Department, USGS, out in Salt Lake City. Only has three hundred hours on it. Brand new airplane."

"Well, write a letter."

I said, "Letter, heck. Let's telephone them."

"Telephone is expensive, Ralph. We don't even know who to talk to."

I says, "Well, you suppose we could afford a two-dollar telegram? Because everybody will be wanting this airplane."

He said, "Well, write up a telegram, and we'll send it out." I wrote it up, said we'd send a licensed pilot out for it. When I went out there to pick up the airplane, they said, "You were the only one to send a telegram. These agencies around Utah and Nevada, they took a day. One of them walked in the next morning. We said, 'We already got a telegram.'"

So we got the first airplane for the Park Service, a 1955 single-engine, 150 horsepower, two-place airplane. It had tandem wheels for landing in soft muddy stuff. I flew that airplane 3,500 hours. I've still got the logbook. I was featured with that plane in *Life* magazine about '59. But in 1960, at Sirtilly Farms, where we kept the plane for a while, some local no-goodniks broke in, stole the engine and a prop, and burned the whole hangar.

That's when we got the Lake. We used the Lake for everything you can imagine. Law enforcement. Biological research. Eagle nests, osprey nests, spoonbill nests, great white herons. Used it for counting turtles' nests on the beaches, counting manatees from the air. Fire control, flying VIPs, orientation for park personnel. Boat counts. Monitoring commercial fishing, traps, nets, hook-and-line fishermen. I was flying pretty much every day. Got to spend eight hours in ninety to one hundred-degree temperatures at low altitude, rough and bumpy. I'd come down and my shirts would be brown instead of gray. Still, I loved my job. Because it was so different.

Most of the time there was somebody with me, like Dr. Robertson, John Ogden, Oron "Sonny" Bass. Those guys have flown with me for hours on bird counts. We monitored over fifty eagle nests, from early fall until late spring, until the young were all fledged out. This was at the time when DDT was causing problems. We knew where every nest was.

We were also looking at herons, and the great white herons were really a study because we would find a white-blue pair. Seemed like every ornithologist from all over the world was here to fly with me to see a white-blue pair and waiting to see what the offspring were, if they could reproduce. I don't think anybody ever got the answer to that one.

Prior to Hurricane Donna we had a bird census. Two weeks after, we had another census. Some of the ibis colonies south of Chokoloskee were practically wiped out. You could see feathers and carcasses on the mangroves. No leaves on those trees, they were all blown off.

We used the airplane for the Christmas bird counts, and we counted birds that people didn't see on the ground. Like black-necked stilts. A lot of those. I got flamingoes one time, off Snake Bight and off southern Lake Ingraham. And then a scarlet ibis with a whole bunch of white ibis on the flats above Bear Lake. And then I had to fly first one and then the other saying, "Scarlet ibis? No way. Miele, you lie." I had to fly them so they could see for themselves and, of course, put it on their life list.

Then we started counting manatees from the air. One of them, north of Everglades City in the Ten Thousand Islands, was always there. It had big red blotches on it. Every winter it was in that same area, always with one or two others. Everybody wanted to see it.

Then there were the turtle crawls. On early morning flights, low tide, we'd fly right along the beach, and in ten minutes of flight they could tell how many turtle crawls were there. They would mark them on a map, then go by boat, see which ones the raccoons had dug up or if people had been there to dig up the eggs.

We've seen leatherbacks from the air, and on the beach we've seen loggerheads, greens, and tortoise shells. After Donna, I kept seeing this one turtle inland, so I put the rangers out there, and it was a Ridley, a rare Ridley. It couldn't seem to get out of that Bear Lake and canal area, back to the Gulf. So they took it and then released it in Florida Bay.

I was up in Georgia with the airplane when Hurricane Donna was still coming up. I decided to fly over the mountains to save the airplane. So I've filed a flight plan, I'm waiting for clearance, and I got the juke radio on. They say that Donna has crossed the peninsula and gone out into the Atlantic. So I changed my flight plan to come south, and I had fifty mile per hour tail winds. That plane had a five-hour tank. I gassed it in Lakeland. Then, on the park radio, they said, "Fly over Everglades City, see what's left over there."

So I did. The rangers in the townhouse there, on the balcony, said, "Land!" Well, the airport there was awash in mud and trees all over. I said, "No way." I flew on to my airstrip at Sirtilly's. It was under water and that's where the gas was. I needed gas. So I landed on the Main Park Road, taxied to the parking lot at headquarters, and they brought me aviation gas.

In the first two weeks after Donna, I bet I flew two hundred hours. It seemed like every scientist wanted to fly. Dr. Craighead wanted to see every tree that was down.

Another thing we did with the airplanes, fire control. And poachers. There's fires in the mangroves, sometimes by lightning strikes, but often by poachers' match strikes. I flew sometimes day, sometimes night searching for gator poachers. Deer poachers too. Caught a lot of them. I'd see something going on, talk to the guys on the ground.

And we had a lot of stop-netting. There's a lot of creeks and rivers up in the mangroves. So these guys would put a net across the mouth of the river. As the tide goes down, the fish get caught in the net. They'd pick out what was salable, and the rest would go to waste. Terrible, terrible. I remember one time up off Island Point. They had stop-netted it and the net was laying on the ground, and there was about one hundred permit, all dead. Permit was preserved as a game fish, so they couldn't take it. They didn't expect the airplane to come over. I caught them red-handed.

I've watched from the air, so-called mullet fishermen, but they were taking everything else—mangrove snappers, shad, whatever got in the net. When the blue crabs would come up, they would smash 'em, shake 'em out. They'd say they were only taking the mullet and the rest of the fish were going back in. Well, the rest of the fish were dead.

Back in those days the park was still in the land acquisition process. The land acquisition guy, Al Manly, died, and then Bob Schenker, the surveyor, left. And I got the files, all the abstracts, all the maps. I became the liaison between the superintendent's office and the land acquisition office.

So, I'm going through these files one at a time. At Key West, they would have a deed for a piece of land people had been paying on for years. Land sellers had made these beautiful full-color brochures talking about Massachusetts Avenue, Connecticut Avenue, "nearby schools and shopping centers, hospitals." They'd have a brochure with a picture of a couple, he's got a fishing rod and she's knitting or mending nets, and a palm tree over here, you know. So a couple that has been paying on property for years goes to Key West, and they ask, "Can you tell us where our property is?"

"Well, it's somewhere north of Lostmans River. You'll have to go to the National Park Service. They'll tell you where it is." So I've had them come out to the park, and I'd have to tell them, "It's under water. There are no roads. Nearest survey line is more than twenty miles away. It has never been surveyed. You can't get there." And they cried. They'd bought this land that was nothing but water and mangroves.

We needed a new airplane, a second airplane. We had been renting a Grummon Widgeon, a six-place amphibious aircraft, you know, Widgeon like a duck. This particular Widgeon was built in 1945, last of the line, serial #1245. They only made 1,500 of them. The Lake was four-place, single-engine. This Widgeon was six-place, twin-engine.

I wore out two sets of engines in it. I put over three thousand hours just flying that airplane in Everglades and between Everglades and Fort Jefferson and Biscayne. I flew that plane until 1980 when I retired. I hear that it's now in the Navy museum in Pensacola.

In the Widgeon, I flew the House Appropriations Committee to Fort Jefferson by way of the Big Cypress. A lot of birds, roosts, and rookeries. We were working on Big Cypress at the time. The estimate for buying all the lands within the proposed boundary of Big Cypress was $105 million. Cheap. So I had five of them in the airplane coming back, and I'm telling them they need the Big Cypress to keep it from being developed. "You know all that shrimp you were eating out at Fort Jefferson? Those shrimp come from the Gulf of Mexico." I said, "The shrimp landing for the Keys area of the state of Florida last year was $23 million. And there is a factor, I'm told, by economists, of about sixteen. That means that that was the price for the shrimp that were sold. But they have boats that go out and get it. They have to have fuel. They have to have food. They have to have ice, equipment, nets. The shrimp comes into a packing house. They are sorted, packaged, transported by truck, by airplane. So they have to have boxes, they have to have ice. So there was a factor of sixteen just for shrimp. And that's only one of about twenty-five different varieties of fish that depend on this fresh water flowing down through Big Cypress. The shrimp spend their juvenile life cycle in that warm brackish water of the mangroves. They spend three or four months there, grow to about an inch or an inch and a half, and then they migrate out."

Roy Chandler says, "Well, Ralph, that's fine. But how am I going to tell my constituents in North Carolina that I want $105 million worth of taxes to buy land in Florida to protect your fisheries?"

"I'm glad you asked that, Mr. Chairman, because it's not just our fisheries in Florida. How many times have you gone out to catch channel bass off your shores in North Carolina? Ever fished off the Outer Banks?"

"Oh, yes, all the time."

"Ever catch any tuna out there?"

"Yes."

"Where are those tuna now?"

"They're not there. That's why I'm not out there fishing."

I said, "They're feeding in the Gulf of Mexico."

"What are they feeding on?"

"They are feeding on the shrimps, the crabs, the mullet, other crustaceans."

Midland, Texas, comes on. "Well," he says, "up in Midland we got oil wells. What am I going to tell my people?"

I said, "Did you ever hear of Corpus Christie, Texas? Galveston? Aransas Pass?"

"Oh, yes," he says. "That's Texas."

"Half of those shrimp boats you saw out there on the Gulf are from Texas."

He said, "Mr. Chairman, I'll buy in."

Happy Chandler said, "Me too, I'm Oklahoma, and we don't have . . . "

I said, "Wait a minute."

He said, "Never mind, Ralph. Yes."

They passed it. The appropriations bill. It was only $105 million.

I loved my job. It was just so different. When I retired, I was told by a lot of people, "Nobody lives more than ten years after they're retired." I've been retired thirty years. I went fishing yesterday. It was a beautiful day on the water.

Bright mangrove channels open a world of water and sky. Photograph by Anne McCrary Sullivan

Rick Horton and Wanda Townsend en route to Fakahatchee Island. Photograph by Holly Genzen.

RETURN TO FAKAHATCHEE

Wanda Brown Townsend

CHOKOLOSKEE PIONEER

At the age of eighty, Wanda Brown Townsend took a kayak trip from Everglades City to Fakahatchee Island where her grandparents and other family members had lived when she was a child. This was her first trip to Fakahatchee in approximately fifty years. Her neighbor, Rick Horton, facilitated the trip and provided paddle power for her kayak. The authors, Holly and Anne, made this paddle alongside Rick and Wanda. Wanda was equipped with a digital recorder and a clip-on microphone.

Wanda: Well, now, I didn't live out there. It was my people. I just went down and visited. We would go to my grandpa and grandmother's place, stay two or three days, then go over and stay with my cousins, with Uncle Phinnes and Aunt Ada. I'd stay down there a week at a time, you know. It was great. You want me to get in this kayak?

Rick: Yes ma'am. Put your hand on my shoulder.

Wanda: I told Virginia, I said, "Don't look for me at prayer meeting tonight, I won't be there." She said, "What're you gonna do?" I said, "I'm going to Fakahatchee! Kayaking." She said, "Kayaking?!" They just can't believe that I would even kayak. Not even my brother. I'm going to call him when I get back. I've got it made. I don't have to paddle. I turned over in one of these things one time.

Rick: You're not going to turn over today.

Wanda: You know, Uncle Phinnes and Aunt Ada always seemed elderly to me. But you couldn't tell it in their actions. They didn't have too much of an education, but they knew how to work and get by, let me tell you. They had cows. We would make our own butter. Aunt Ada had a big churn for hers, but she'd give us girls a quart jar and we'd sit in a chair and shake those quart jars, make our butter.

Grandpa, he made a long table and a bench in behind it for us children. We'd sit there, and we couldn't wait for grandmother to milk a cow, bring the milk in, and we'd drink it warm. They always cooked on a wooden stove. That's what we called it, a wooden stove. They had good food back there.

Curlews would fly over, and we would kill a mess of them and bring 'em in, cook 'em up right then. And young cranes, you could go out at night when they come in to roost, kill them just with a stick, bring 'em in, cook 'em up. They was really good. More tender than the curlews. I mean, the white curlews, you know, that's the old ones, they was so tough you have to stew them, make gravy on 'em. If you get the brown ones, you can fry them, but they're still tough to me. It's been a long time since I've eat anything like that. Can't do it anymore.

All the bread was homemade. We used to call them Johnnie Hookers. Cooked on the iron griddle. You have to cook 'em so slow, make sure the middle is done. Cause they're thick. Uncle Flinn and Aunt Ada's daughter could really cook 'em, and she'd cook a big old pot of lima beans. Aunt Ada had about eleven children. My grandmother had eleven.

Rick: Tell us about the polio out here.

Wanda: Most of the children at Fakahatchee had polio. There was a girl, Vernelle. She was crippled up with it. And then there was Johnnie, and J. P. They was crippled with it. Ruth had a little bit of it. And all of them, they just barely could get around and help their selves.

I was in swimming down there one time, Phleany and I, and we'd take a little boat, and we'd play gator around it. We'd swim under the boat, you know, and hide and all. When we were bringing the boat back to the dock, well, they had a anchor on the front of it, and you'd throw the anchor over the dock, and I did, and it hit me and busted my lip wide open. Vernelle was sitting on the porch, and she says, "Oh, Wanda's bleedin'! She's dyin'!" And Aunt Ada run out there and she took me over by the cistern and rinsed me all off, and took me in the house and stuck a handkerchief in camphor, and she said, "Just hold this to your mouth." So I did, and she rinsed it out with salt water. I had a little lump there for a long time, you could feel it with your finger.

It's been a long time since I've seen an oyster bar. I think that one over there would cut your feet up, wouldn't it?

Rick: Well, now, how did Totch and the rest of those kids day-to-day walk on oyster bars with bare feet?

Wanda: I don't know. There used to be a man named Chisolm Rivers walked barefooted on oyster bars. They said he never wore shoes. He bought him a pair at Sears and Roebuck and walked out with them over his shoulder. That's what they said.

My brother, Jiggs, used to get good oysters off of them mangrove roots. Raccoons liked to eat 'em too. Later, my husband, James, and I would go down and get oysters that was in deep water, right on the sand, and we would tong 'em. Oh, they was large oysters!

Rick: Now, how did that whole Daniels gang out here go to church?

Wanda: My grandpa and grandmother is the onliest ones that I know about that went to church down Fakahatchee. But Johnny used to love it when he came over to

Chokoloskee. He loved church. He was on crutches, and he would just have to pull hisself and, you know, jump, all the way across that island. Back then, we only had cow paths, just little old roads. It was great, though, I tell you, that island Chokoloskee was. We didn't have anything, but you know, we didn't really know it. Us kids. And, yeah, we all sang. Most of the songs we sang, even outside of church, was hymns. Old songs.

Rick: Tell us about turtle-turning on Cape Romano.

Wanda: You call it Cape Romano, we call it Cape Ro*man*. I went with my aunt and uncle for turtle-turning. We cooked 'em out there. My Aunt Lavinia, she could cook the best turtle soup on them open fires. We had boyfriends and sometimes a group of us would get together and go. We walked the beach, all night, you know, looking for turtles. Every turtle that we seen on the beach, we turned. In the morning, the boys would pick them up and put 'em in the boat. When you turn 'em over, then they can't get back upright, you know.

Sometimes we went turtling on Chokoloskee. It was a shell mound, and it was real tall. We'd sit on top of that and watch them come across the water and lay their eggs on the land. And we would gather the eggs. Aunt Annie Bramon, Mama's sister, would give us a quarter a egg for 'em. With our loggerhead turtle eggs, they're very large, my sister made cakes. Some people really liked the turtle eggs and they'd boil them and eat 'em. But I never did eat an egg. I ate turtles. They're good.

Rick: That's Fakahatchee over there, behind that island. You see all the naked branches of the gumbo limbos there? That little white spot is where we're going to put in. But we got another big white spot that's behind this end of the island. I think that's where Aunt Ada and Uncle Phinnes's house was.

Wanda: Right straight ahead of us! We're almost there!

Rick: We'll put in at that white spot, then walk on the trail to this other spot. The cemetery is in between.

Wanda: Rick, you know more about it than I do now, I think.

Rick: I might know what it is now, but I don't know what it *was*. That's the important part. There, off to your right. That's where the houseboat was, isn't it?

Wanda: Oh, you mean when little James fell over and drownded. I don't know exactly where, but between there and the island, that's where Aunt Phleamon and Uncle Jesse had their houseboat.

Rick: I'm going to get out first. And then I'll get you out.

Wanda: Gracious! There is a place where somebody made a fire. It looks like somebody camps every now and then. My brother said there's a path, but I don't know where it's at. It's so growed up.

Rick: We'll have to walk around and let me show you. We'll eat here when we get back.

Wanda: Well, we'll see where we wind up at. Rick's the leader. *Whooo*! Cactus, cactus. Boy, it's been a long time since I've seen these sticker pears. We used to take the fruit from it, when we were kids, we would take soap and foam it up and color it with the fruit. We'd make mud pies and that was our icing.

A WALK THROUGH FAKAHATCHEE ISLAND

Wanda: It's the cemetery! There's Vernell. She was the one that I said was sitting on the porch when I came out of the water. She could walk but not straight like us. She would always sit with her legs crossed under her in the chair. She was just sitting all the time. But she could embroidery.

Who's this, last name of Sands? It must've been something to do with Aunt Ada. He died in '33. I was born in 1933.

And, look, there's Frances. I didn't know she was buried on this island. I thought she was buried in Naples. She was older, you know, and had moved away.

And here's Uncle Phinnes.

Rick: That's a nice stone, a pretty one. Looks like a rose, and it says, *Father, gone but not forgotten*.

Wanda: That's my mother's brother. And here's James Phinnes Daniels Jr., that fell off from the houseboat and drownded.

Here's a Brown. He was two years old. '42–'44. That was Frances and Boss's son. He was sick for a few days down at Chokoloskee. And he died. They think that maybe he ate something poison.

That one was Aunt Ada's mother, Aunt Ginny Knowles. She was the one that would get mad with Phleany and I when we were sitting in the breezeway. We'd be talking and laughing, and she didn't want to hear that. She'd come out of that room and, boy, she'd get onto us!

Edward Clifton Anderson. You know what? That must have been Doris's husband, Uncle Phinnes's daughter. I didn't know that he was buried out here. There's a lot that I really don't know about this graveyard.

Rick: Well it's gonna be fifty years since you were out here. This trail over here goes to a home site. What's that tree, Wanda?

Wanda: Sapodilla. Sapodilla tree. We used to be climbing all up in there to eat that fruit and Uncle Phinnes would say, "Now don't ya'll be breaking them limbs."

One of these cisterns is where Uncle Phinnes kept a big gator. Fleeney and I would come down here and pester it to hear it beller. Oh! This cistern's almost full.

Rick: This is a very tight cistern. It's great workmanship.

Wanda: Living here must've been very hard. But they did it. And to them, it probably wasn't hard. Now, that looks like one of them wash pots that they used to use, one of them boil pots. They'd do their wash, boil their clothes and then rub them on a rub board. I did it once or twice and rubbed all the knuckles off my hand. Mama had a big old iron boil pot, had legs on it. It took Mama half a day to put out a wash.

Rick: That path there is the way we'll go back. See, the beach is just right over there.

Wanda: You know, there hasn't been any bugs today. The weather, I think. I hope they stay where they are, don't find us.

Rick: It's been a long time since they've tasted Brown blood out here. They could have a feast.

Wanda: I know. They'd say, "How'd you ever get back on this island?" Some crazy man from LaBelle drug me out here.

Rick: We gotta go get some lunch!

Wanda: Yeah! We got to get some energy up. Follow the leader! You're going to have to pull me up that slope, Rick, if'n you don't fall down it too.

Rick: That way goes back to the boat, but we're going to take a look at the dump first.

Wanda: Boy, look at the jars there. And that's the tree you don't want to get into. Burn 'em out, and when that's burning, it will swell you up like I don't know what, if the smoke's blowing on you. I don't know what it's called. We had 'em on Chokoloskee. White milky stuff comes out of it.

Rick: There's some crockery here. Look, it's real pretty, like a base of a cake plate, with roses and stuff. Somebody cried when this got broken. You just didn't go out to the local oyster bar and find another one of those, did you?

Fakahatchee Island, Wanda Townsend and Rick Horton. Photograph by Anne McCrary Sullivan.

LUNCH ON FAKAHATCHEE

Wanda: We're going to need some plates out of the bag and some forks. I think I brought everything. Napkins. Now, you all have some of this meat, and guess what it is. It's venison.

Rick: Wanda wants to be sure we all have energy and can get back. The only way Wanda gets back is if we all get back! It's probably been fifty, sixty, seventy years since somebody's eaten venison on Fakahatchee Island.

Wanda: That's right. And we've got plenty of potato salad.

Anne: Wanda, when you picture your mama, what do you see her doing?

Wanda: Just housewife. All we children had was school and church, and she was just home. She took care of us and visited in the neighborhood, you know. She made all of my school clothes. I couldn't wait for her to make me a new dress! We had them big bows in the back, you know, that tied, great big wide bows.

Rick: *Only* a housewife. She cooked all the meals, cleaned up after everybody, washed all the clothes, probably made all the clothes.

Wanda: Only mine.

Rick: Where did James get his?

Wanda: Catalog. Order 'em. Sears and Roebuck. Montgomery Ward. And Albans.

Rick: How come he got his clothes from the catalog?

Wanda: Cause Mama didn't make 'em. But in my early teens, Jiggs, he'd say, "Wanda, make me out a order," and then he'd tell me what he wanted, and then he'd let *me* order something. Every time I made out a order I always got a dress. Anybody want some more? Eat all you want.

Rick: I've never had any venison this tender before. Wanda has cooked me up some alligator this way. She puts it through a little sort of macerator, and that makes it very tender.

Wanda: The Indians used to camp around on Chokoloskee island, you know. I was just a kid, and you know, you read books. And I was so scared of 'em. We had to walk to the post office to get the mail every day. I'd tip-toe, I'd be real quiet going around them Indians 'cause I thought they was goin' to get me. And almost to the post office, at that corner, they was always camping there and they always had a big iron pot cooking something, stirring it with a big wooden spoon. I would just slip by them. And then I'd try to slip back by, come the back way. Oh, I was scared of them.

I tell you when the road come across from Everglades to Chokoloskee, the people that came in would dig that place up looking for Indian artifacts. To us, it didn't mean nothing. We were just living there. And I'd be sneaking by them Indians real quiet thinking they wouldn't see us and right out there in the open. They wouldn't have hurt us. They were good people. I should've stopped by and eat lunch with them where they were making their soup in that big old pot out on an open fire.

Did y'all get enough food?

LEAVING FAKAHATCHEE

Wanda: Look how rough looking it is over there. We're fixin' to get in some rough water.

Rick: I think once we get out there it won't be so bad. But this may be one of our windier bays. Maybe we'll get up to that bar by Ferguson River and have another lemon cookie.

Wanda: Once, one of my friends and I, after we got through trout fishing and was coming home, every place that we would take, the trees would run together, and we got lost. One of our friends from Chokoloskee, Robert Smallwood, he had a party he was guiding, and we had to go over and ask him how to get back home! "Oh, my goodness, I can't believe, Chokoloskee girls that can't find their way back home!" We was so embarrassed. But you know, we'd get going and we'd come to a stop. We'd go another way and come to another stop. All of 'em looked alike. Them mangroves, it looks like all of them run together. You can't find a way. We had fun, though. And after he told us, we made it back.

[Landing at the oyster bar] Rick's got to get out the cookies! This is a nice bar. A lonely bird every now and then, flying by their self. We're not too far from Chokoloskee now.

Do you have Totch Brown's book? He was my first cousin. They all had a good life back here. I've never known 'em for complaining. Would you like to go see his island? Totch's daughter, Lorna, owns it now. She used to go out there by herself and stay, and she'd want me to come out there and stay, and my son would say, "I'd take you out there, Mama," but I never did go. Lorna. Lorna Rewis.

When James and I was married and living on a houseboat, Lorna and Raymond came to us and wanted James to drive them across the state to get married. He wouldn't do it. He didn't want Totch and Estelle against him. Lorna was young, maybe fifteen, maybe fourteen, and she was running away. So we didn't do it. I don't know how they got married. But they did get married. They're still married.

Now, can you imagine buying an island like this out here? Wonder how come Totch figured out coming over here and camping on that island.

View from Fakahatchee Island.
Photograph by Anne McCrary
Sulliuvan.

Rick: Maybe he had some leftover drug money. He knew he wasn't going to take it with him. Did he get much of a chance to enjoy it, or did he die before . . .

Wanda: He got a chance.

TOTCH'S ISLAND

Wanda: [Reading a small sign] *This is a private island, recorded in the Collier County tax office. Lorna and Eddie Rewis. Please respect.* I don't know if Lorna comes out here now or not. Look at the wood piled up. Crab trap. Even got a hammock up in the tree. Y'all want to look inside? It's not locked.

Letter from Lorna: *This is my little home. It's not for public use. It's hard to come back each time and find it abused. It's abused enough by the lizards. God protect it. Watch over it with your watchful eye. Totch's daughter, Lorna.*

Wanda: Lorna was going to finish Totch's second book, but she must not've.

Rick: The amazing part is that at one time Wanda had the *original* manuscript for his first book.

Wanda: It was real thick.

Rick: He only used maybe a third of that manuscript.

Wanda: Yeah, because they couldn't.

Rick: In the whole drug running part of it, he really named names. They left it all out of the first book. In that book, he says, "You know, I always wanted to do one good run." It was like, well, he never really got that run.

Wanda: I loaned it to my neighbor and never gotten it back, and it's been years. Let's write a note to Lorna and stick it up there.

Dear Lorna. I went to Fakahatchee with some good friends. On the way back, we stopped by to see your house. It is beautiful. We wish you had been here. Love, Wanda.

Why don't you all sign it too?

Rick: All we have to do now is paddle across Chokoloskee Bay.

Wanda: It's a roarin'. Good thing we don't get seasick!

When you go to Chokoloskee, look for Townsend Lane. Straight down that road to the water was my place. A canal on each side of me and a waterfront. It was one of the best places on the island. I lived on Chokoloskee fifty-seven years. I was born on that island. I didn't leave till there wasn't nothing else for me to do down there. My husband got where he wasn't able to crab anymore, so we moved to LaBelle. James always wanted to move to LaBelle. Always. And when he went out of crabbing, there wasn't nothing else left for us to do. Most of my people has moved away from Chokoloskee. But I know a few that says when they moved, it would be in a box. And I believe it.

The young shark's world. Photograph by JohnBob Carlos.

THE AWAKENING

JohnBob Carlos

PHOTOGRAPHER AND ENVIRONMENTAL ACTIVIST

My grandmother before she passed, she said, "You've been going back there into those areas a lot."

I said, "Yes."

She said, "It's in your blood."

I said, "What do you mean?"

She said, "Some of your family was from Florida and they left to Cuba. It's full circle now. You're returning back to where you have ancestry. The Indians that were in Cuba used to travel back and forth. And some of the indigenous folks there in Cuba are mixed into our family."

I've always felt this affinity for the Everglades. I feel like, on some of those islands where the shell works were done, there's people still out there, watching. There were stories and songs, and I can almost hear them. Some of the islands back in Everglades National Park have mounds, and there are certain areas, you feel they're sacred. I've run into artifacts, blades, and things from indigenous folks. I try not to touch them 'cause in my culture it's bad to touch or move anything from the past.

That methane smell, for me, coming off the mud, I start smelling that and I get anxious to get out on the water. It's almost like a state for me, and all these good memories start rolling back into my head. My family is second generation Floridians. We didn't have much money. And so my stepfather and my mom, before this coastal area was developed, we'd drive, every weekend. Back then it was simple. We would sleep in the car, eat sandwiches. My stepfather was a Vietnam vet. He was always a little bit haunted about that. The only place where he seemed to feel tranquil, the place where he was happiest was out here. That's the place where my whole family was most happy. No matter how hard it was at home, if there wasn't much food or if work was hard. It was a sanctuary, not only for animals, but a sanctuary for myself, for all of us.

That was the start for me. Later on, when I was sixteen, seventeen, I was fishing and camping, finding every little nook and pond that I could hop into and explore. I didn't have a map, and I didn't know anyone that had ever been out there. When I went to Everglades National Park, and I saw the sign for Hells Bay, I said, "Let's do it!" I went with two bottles of water, in shorts and a T-shirt, and paddled, learning things on the way: you need to take more water, take more maps. As I grew, I started exploring deeper in those mangroves. I'd go in the morning, with that light coming in and the birds. I'd be out there seeing everything wake up. And that was serenity.

In my culture, my Cuban heritage, we believe that when you go through the mangroves or go through any forest, it's a cleaning. There's thousands and thousands of leaves, and each plant takes away a bad thing from you. You have clean air, and you have those trees, and you have the water, and each thing takes something bad away. It almost became an obsession for me to go out there, and at the same time, I was fishing, always following the fish, trying to figure out where does this fish go and how does it live?

Paddling was the best way to get into the mangroves and into good fishing spots. Paddling takes a little bit more work, but you immerse yourself. You get a little bit wet. I got into it, and I had a lot of interest in the Lake Ingraham area and Bear Lake. I mean, that was untouched, unspoiled. What started leading me back there, was old Calusa trails. You start looking at the maps, and you say, "Wait a minute. That trail's carved out." These trails were created, and when the tide was low, you could actually see them.

I'd explore in Bear Lake, and I'd see the white pelicans come in and some of the best flamingo sightings. In November, December, January, ospreys are fighting the eagle for their food. I'd see crocodiles. Their behavior towards you is "What are you?" Oh, man, it's just amazing.

I was very selfish during that period, very into me enjoying it, trying to do all the trails I could, trying to get to the most remote areas. And fishing was heaven out there. So that whole exploring period, I call it the exploring period, from eighteen, twenty-five, thirty years old, I'm focused on myself. I wanted to enjoy this as much as I could.

Then I started finding that fishing was not so important. Getting out there was what mattered. And I realized I had fallen in love. Fishing was okay, but seeing those dolphins play and move around in that water became more important to me. Or seeing those sea turtles or a sawfish in the water. I was finding beautiful orchids and plants, and I started learning about them, like when to go and see the coco orchid in bloom. Little by little, my rod started staying home. I kept taking the camera.

Now, I still love fishing and every once in a while, have that urge, and I'll go out with the rod, go after fish. Then let them go. It's still part of what drives me out here. But there's a deeper connection. Sometimes I'll stand still in those mangroves, and it's not so buggy today, and then I start seeing the little warbler and all these little birds, and I hear that *tat-tat-tat-tat-tat*, and I'm like, "There is magic here." I start seeing the water coming in and the fish. I start *really* seeing. And I think: I could just sit here in this sanctuary. It's beautiful, and the birds are waiting for me. It's a sanctuary for them like it is for me. I forget that I have to go back to my car and my life and how this or that has to be done and so-and-so is in the hospital, and my family has this problem. And I almost feel sometimes, when I am in certain areas, that I'm coming back home. It's not like, um. . . . It's different for me. It's spiritual.

When I had my son, my world started changing. The question popped in my head. Is it going to be around for him? I started going out there and asking, "What's really going on here?" At the same time, I still wanted to get from here to there. I have this inflatable kayak. It's very sturdy. I can carry thirty pounds. I would figure out how to do these crazy trips. I think about Lostmans Pines. And then I think, "Now wait a minute. I fish Lostmans River. Those must connect. Can I paddle my way from here to there and then paddle my way back to the Park?" So I take my water supply, and I inflate this inflatable kayak, and I say to myself, "Are you that crazy, to do this?" And I say, "Yes, you are that crazy." What drives a person to do that sort of thing? I don't know. You really have to love it and want to see.

West Lake is beautiful. You have the Lungs back there, and Gator Lake where the old ranger station is. On the high tide, you can get into the Lost Lakes, and crocodiles are hanging out back there and beautiful little crabs. Those are little jewels of the park. I was really into finding those and watching the weather change.

Say we're in West Lake or Mud Lake or Bear Lake, and I would see a storm coming. In some of these mangrove areas, there are little caves that open up inside. While that rain is coming in and going over you real heavy, if you can make it to one of those little caves, you slip right in and tie up. The mangroves will shelter you, and you'll be okay till that rain passes over and you come back out and paddle on.

Somewhere along the way we started having the internet, and it became important to me to start saying online, "Hey, we have this beautiful, beautiful thing, and it's another world, mystical. . . . I spent nights out there and I saw the dolphins, the way they communicate. It was almost human." And I was posting fishing reports.

I started looking at links between Big Cypress and Everglades National Park's mangrove areas. Where is this fresh water coming from? Where is it going? It's a moving river, right? October, early September, you're always looking for freshwater flow that comes down from Big Cypress to the mangroves, that water and those nutrients. The way stone crabbers know there's going to be a good stone crab season, it's if enough fresh water is making it in here. They're so tuned to this area that they can go and look at the color of the water, and they can tell you, "It'll be a good stone crab season." I started learning tides. And I joined a group online that was trying to figure out how did things flow.

In my midthirties, I was still doing photos and fishing reports, and a lot of my pictures ended up being crocodiles and orchids and spoonbills, and these guys started saying, "Hey. Your fishing reports are great. Have you thought of going into photography? Your photos are awesome."

If you want to have an interesting day, just go and strand yourself, even down at Flamingo. Or on Little Rabbit Key, magical island. And when you paddle over there, make sure you have an umbrella so you're not hot. Freeze something special to drink or eat on this day. Something good. Something you just want to have. Strand yourself and let the birds come. Just stop.

That's how I got to see the mink up in Fakahatchee Swamp. I'd been chasing after them for months. Usually, I move a lot when I go out doing photography. I gotta get to this point, I gotta get to that point. I said, "I'm going to pick an area and I'm going to go and sit there for a week, see what happens." I would go every day, get there at 7:00 in the morning and leave at 5:00. Every day, I would sit in the same place.

One day I fell asleep, and when I woke up, I felt something on my leg. I thought it was a cottonmouth. I thought, "Don't move." I looked. The mink was standing right on my leg, looking at me. I reached to get my camera and he ran over to his nest, right over there. And I thought to myself, "Are you kidding? I've been sitting here all week, and his nest was right over there." I got videos of him, and then I came back and finished out the week there. I did get to see a cottonmouth. A cottonmouth came in and those little fish were in the water, and the cottonmouth was just feasting on them. I got to see it eating.

I've been lost out there sometimes, even stranded. I was out on Joe River in a motorboat one night with my brother. We'd gone twenty-five miles through Joe River all the way down to Whitewater Bay. It was choppy, and a rogue wave hit our boat.

I start making my way to shore, but the boat's so full of water that it's trying to capsize, and the motor is done for. So we wait a couple of hours until the wind changes direction. We start paddling and moving with the tide. It was peaceful. I was in heaven because I knew I was getting to stay out there longer. As we're paddling, it starts getting more and more choppy. I say, "Okay, it's getting dark. We'll work our way back tomorrow. We're going to find an island for tonight."

I didn't have a radio or a GPS, but when we didn't get back, my wife called the park and talked to a ranger. He said, "We know that guy, JohnBob, he's okay. He's probably out in the Hells Bay area. In the morning, I'll go out and get him." In the morning, Tony Terry came out for us. We had to leave the boat out there.

I brought my wife with me to pick up the boat. I told the captain that was taking us out, "Don't point out any crocodiles." The guy had a sense of humor. "Crocodile." "Crocodile." "There's another crocodile." My wife was pregnant then, and she said, "You'll never bring our son here! Look at that crocodile! You're never going to bring our son here."

So when he's around three years old, we're going down the same canal. I was a lot safer then. I had radio and GPS. I got more mature. And I also got a beating from some of the old timers, telling me, "You know, you go really deep trips. You need to start taking these things with you."

So I was at home out there, and it was beautiful, and then I had my kid, and like I said, things started changing for me. I started bringing him out here. And I started to see a decline. I called it like an empty museum. I wasn't seeing a lot of animals. Something was starting to really feel wrong.

Then I had something I call the Awakening. It was like someone slapped me, "Hey! You need to wake up and pay attention, and you need to get out there and look at what's going on." My tribal friend Houston's words to me were, "Marjory Stoneman Douglas." He asked me, "What have you done for the Everglades lately?" Here I was, passionate about the Everglades, talking about all these areas, how to get there. And I couldn't answer. I said, "What do you mean?" I got aggravated, actually angry. I went home, and I thought about it, and I thought, "Right. I haven't done anything."

I saw how beautiful areas, like certain domes along the Tamiami, were being turned into parking lots where I used to see rare orchids right off the road. I started seeing fish kills and algae blooms off the beaches. We had people wanting to drill for oil, people wanting to cut out huge chunks of the mangroves, and water was having some major issues. And I started understanding. It was a gradual thing. No one pieced it together for me. That was all part of the Awakening.

Fire in the sky. Photograph by JohnBob Carlos.

I started praying before going into the woods, started praying for the woods, started asking permission before going in. I would ask permission from folks actually there with me and also from folks that may still be there, ask them to help me, protect me, guide me. I would say that I came just to look, enjoy, and respect.

I started asking, "Why are we doing this?" And that was the Awakening. I said, "This has to stop." I thought to myself, "Have I been only receiving all this time?"

I started focusing on taking these photos, images of areas I had learned from fishing and exploring. When I do photography, if something captures me, it's like electricity. The electricity gets me, and it pulls me. When that happens, I'm connected. I'm seeing it and feeling it and hearing it. For one brief instant, I'm connected to the past, the present, the future. That's where those photos come from. And that has changed me a lot.

I wanted to get more educated. I would go to meetings and hear people talking about places they'd never seen—but I had seen them. I knew even those pumps they were talking about. Things started coming together for me. So this is why this area is destroyed; they're pumping out water. I started realizing that money was so important to people here in Florida that we didn't care about the future.

I looked at my son and said, "What am I leaving him?" And then I asked myself, "What *have* I done to protect it? What have I done to show people what I've seen?" I hadn't done anything. That's the urgency. The Awakening. I'm Awake. I had been selfish. I had been enjoying every piece of it, going out there and enjoying the birds and enjoying the fish, enjoying the water.

Sometimes I hear people talking about these places, and they're just names or points on a map to them. They're talking, and what I'm seeing in my head are flashes of all these beautiful spots. And so I've started fighting to preserve what we have. I mean, if I die, I've seen it. I've enjoyed it. But you know what? When I go, if this would be still here, I can go in peace. But if I die, and I know that I didn't do anything to protect this, and it's gone. . . .

My son says, "I don't want you to die, Dad."

I say, "I'm okay with that, son, that's part of life." I say, "If you want to see me, you can always come here. You'll feel me as that breeze flows on your shoulder. That's me. You catch that sunset there, and it's the same sunset that we shared. You go and you watch those orchids. I am there. With you. We are looking at the same thing. We're breaking time, we're breaking space, we're breaking everything because we have that common denominator."

A lot of folks don't understand why I'm so vocal. They think I'm crazy. It's not that I'm crazy. We're at the point where we have to understand that it's all connected, and every idea we come up with, we have to analyze it. I don't always see that happening.

My son asks me, "Why do you speak up for these things? Why do you care so much about that tree or those plants or those mangroves?"

I say, "Son. Because it doesn't have a voice. Somebody has to give it a voice." He doesn't get it. But one day he will.

So here we are at Smallwood Store. Where we're at is why we're here, right at the edge of the mangroves. You know, I'm not the smartest man. I'm not the best well written. I'm not even the best photographer. I shoot. And some of the photo shoots I've done

out there, I'm crying like a baby. I mean, having to shoot in an area that I know is going to be destroyed. And I have to figure out how to capture . . .

Even the Spaniards when they came and wrote on their maps *Laguna del Espiritu Santo*, they knew something here was special. We need to preserve at least some of it. I saw in the newspaper somebody wanted to build a fast track over the marsh. We don't need train systems going through the Everglades. I mean, some places aren't meant to be like Disney World. We already have Disney World.

When I had the Awakening, I started seeing animals again. To me that meant, "We're still here." Flamingoes, bears . . . the last few years I've seen a lot of owls. They're still here, they're waiting for us. I have faith.

This started as a very selfish journey. Then I started leaving the rod behind and picking up the camera. Eventually, I started using the images to try to help it, to try to take care of it. I believe in God. And I don't even consider myself a photographer. I consider myself a fan. All I do is go and let Him do his job and take a picture of His work. So people can see it and be amazed and appreciate. Cause a lot of us are just running. We are stuck in our homes and stuck in our lives. Before you know it, it's gone.

We're the smartest creatures on the planet. We can think right from wrong. Yet we're the ones that do wrong for everything else here. A bird flies 'cause it flies. A fish eats, and it swims, and it does what it needs to do. We're the creatures on the planet, the other animals, that don't realize what their job is. We have to preserve. We're at a time where we have to.

This has been the story of finding a place to save myself. And now having to save the place. This is the place that saved me, and now I am trying to save it. I have a sense of urgency.

BIBLIOGRAPHY

Brown, Loren G. *Totch: A Life in the Everglades*. Gainesville: University Press of Florida, 1993.

Bryant, Nelson. "99-Mile Wilderness Is Open from Flamingo to Everglades City," *New York Times*, February 19, 1970.

Choate, Ernest A. *The Dictionary of American Bird Names*, rev. ed. Boston, MA: Harvard Common Press, 1985.

Dimock, A.W. and Julian A. *Florida Enchantments*. New York: Outing Publishing Company, 1908.

Dr. Seuss [Theodor Seuss Geisel]. *Oh, The Places You'll Go!* New York: Random House, 1990.

Gamow, George. *A Planet Called Earth*. New York: Viking Books, 1963.

——. *A Star Called the Sun*. New York: Bantam Books, 1965.

Genzen, Holly, and Sullivan, Anne McCrary. *Paddling the Everglades Wildness Waterway*. Birmingham, AL: Menasha Ridge Press, 2011.

Grunwald, Michael. *The Swamp: The Everglades, Florida, and the Politics of Paradise*. New York: Simon & Schuster, 2006.

Hammer, Roger. *Exploring Everglades National Park and the Surrounding Area: A Guide to Hiking, Biking, Paddling, and Viewing Wildlife in the Region*. 2nd ed. Guilford, CT: Falcon Guides, 2015.

Hrdlicka, Arles. *Anthropology of Florida*, 2nd ed. Classics Southeast Archaeology. Tuscaloosa: University of Alabama Press, 2007.

Moore, Clarence Bloomfield. *The West and Central Florida Expeditions of Clarence Bloomfield Moore*. Tuscaloosa: University of Alabama Press, 1999.

National Park Service, US Department of the Interior. *Wilderness Trip Planner*. http://www.nps.gov/ever/planyourvisit/Wilderness-Trip-Planner.

Sears, William H. "The Turner River Site, Collier County, Florida." *The Florida Anthropologist* 9, no.2 (June 1956): 47–60. http://ufdc.ufl.edu/UF00027829/00122.

Tebeau, Charlton. *The Story of Chokoloskee Bay Country*. Miami: Florida Flair Books, 1976.

Truesdell, William G. *A Guide to the Wilderness Waterway of the Everglades National Park*. Coral Gables, FL: University of Miami Press, 1969.

ABOUT THE VOICES AND AUTHORS

THE VOICES

Oron "Sonny" Bass grew up in South Florida where the mangroves were an endless source of discovery and adventure. He fished, explored, learned, and ultimately made a career of the wild outdoors. Recently retired from his career in Everglades National Park, his memories of the mangroves span decades. He was interviewed in his office on Research Road.

John and Donna Buckley, following a career in canoe livery in Michigan, spent thirty-five winters (November–March) on a houseboat in the Everglades mangroves. They assisted with research, search and rescue, paddler assistance, and special projects of the park. They now spend summers volunteering in a remote area of Isle Royale National Park in Lake Superior. They told their story in conversations at Roberts River Chickee, North River Chickee, and on their on their houseboat, *Swamp Lily II*, near Tarpon Bay.

Tom Buttle first experienced the wilderness of Canada as a teenager. His parents would drop him off to spend a month alone in the forest. He now works as a seasonal volunteer in Everglades National Park, always arriving with a kayak in anticipation of solitary paddling and camping in the mangroves. He spoke of his kayaking adventures in his seasonal home in the park on Pine Island.

JohnBob Carlos traces the evolution of his relationship with the natural world of South Florida and notes how his Cuban heritage influences his interactions with the natural world, embracing both ecological and spiritual values. He makes a passionate plea for preservation. He was interviewed on the lower deck of Smallwood Store in Chokoloskee, Florida. (www.johnbobcarlos.com)

Roger Hammer is well-known for his guidebooks and books about wildflowers and botanical features of South Florida. He has spent countless hours, days, and weeks in the mangrove wilderness for a variety of overlapping purposes including plant study, fishing, and solitude. His story is constructed from interviews at his home in Homestead, Florida, and at Coe Visitor Center in Everglades National Park.

Rick Horton, teacher, carpenter, and commercial diver, now explores the mangrove waterways of southwest Florida. He prefers the "edges," where he can more closely observe mangrove communities as they have weathered the passage of time and storm. He particularly notes evidence of human habitation, from early Calusa potsherds and shell mounds to remains of more recent pioneer settlement. Rick shared his stories on the porch of Kapok Cottage, the home he built in LaBelle, Florida.

Leon Howell, a native of South Florida, an outdoorsman since childhood, and a self-professed "science and nature nut," has always chosen work that would get him outside. Following a twenty-year career in the Coast Guard and a second career as charter boat captain, he now revels in his role as interpreter in Everglades National Park. He was interviewed at his home in Homestead, Florida.

Bill Leonard, formerly a professor and faculty advisor to the Whitewater Canoe School at Georgia State, divided his time in retirement between Maine and South Florida. As a member of the Happy Hoofers chapter of Florida Trails, he spent many years paddling in Everglades National Park. He talked with pleasure of his adventures canoeing and clearing trails and also reminisced about solo trips out to single chickees in the mangrove wilderness. Bill was interviewed at a picnic table under a tree on his Maine farm.

John Lewis, having owned an outdoor store in Traverse City, Michigan, has spent many summers at the Ivey House (iveyhouse.com) leading kayak tours out of Everglades City and on the Turner River. In the areas where he paddles, he especially appreciates the diversity of bird life and vegetation and life in the water itself, mixing under the mangroves. He shares this appreciation with the paddlers on his tours. In the summertime he heads "up north," often guiding kayak trips along the coast of Maine. We interviewed John at Ivey House in Everglades City after he returned from a morning kayak tour.

Ralph Miele (1920–2017) flew transport planes in the Pacific during World War II and became the first ranger pilot in the National Park Service. He was initially hired at Everglades National Park in 1952 to work in the fire control tower on Pine Island, but within a few years he was flying for the park—transporting fire control personnel, law enforcement rangers, researchers, politicians, and journalists. He had a bird's-eye view of the complex mangrove estuaries and understood their ecological value. He retired from the Park Service in 1980. He was interviewed in Everglades National Park and at his home on Key Largo.

Constance Mier, a retired professor of exercise physiology at Barry University, has published articles in *Sea Kayaker* on nutrition and on aging, and she won the Fine Arts Award for her entry in the 2015 Audubon Photography Contest. She blogs regularly about her experiences photographing from a canoe. Her interview took place amid the exercise equipment at the lab at Barry University. (www.constancemierphotography.com)

Toby Nipper retired from Florida Power and Light after thirty-nine years of service. He has partici-
pated in paddling races in Michigan and Missouri. As a WaterTribe member, he has been a contestant
the "Florida Challenge," a race from Naples to Key Largo, and also in the "Ultimate Florida Challenge" all the way around the state. With a friend, he has documented a summer thru-paddle of the
Wilderness Waterway (http://www.youtube.com/watch?V=urOXNAjkuoQ). Toby was interviewed at
Gulf Coast Visitor Center in Everglades City just before putting his bimini up and paddling out into
Chokoloskee Bay.

Vivian Oliva, born in Cuba, has been fishing since moving to Miami as a child. Originally working
with a fishing guide in Biscayne Bay, she discovered the waters of Everglades National Park and now
focuses her fishing out of Chockoloskee Bay and the Ten Thousand Islands, angling for snook, triple
tail, and mangrove snapper in the bays and among the mangrove islands. She blogs about her adventures (beachcamper.glogspot.com). Vivian was interviewed at her home via Skype.

Susan Reece worked as an Everglades interpretive ranger and then a supervisory ranger overseeing
activities at Gulf Coast and Shark Valley from 2001–2015. At Gulf Coast, near Everglades City, she
advised paddlers as they planned itineraries and prepared to head out into the mangrove wilderness.
She also oversaw management of the extensive mangrove areas north of the Broad River in Everglades
National Park. Currently, she is chief of interpretation at Pictured Rocks National Lakeshore in
Michigan.

Ann Rougle, on the water since her Annapolis, Maryland, childhood, now has sailing adventures in
a Folbot in Everglades National Park. She values solitude and likes nothing better than to launch into
"magnificent cold fronts." She spends summers traveling and then heads back to the Everglades in the
winter. "If there are past lives," she says, "one of mine was surely as a Calusa. This is my place." Under
the shelter at West Lake in the Everglades, she spoke of her adventures. She keeps a journal and has
shared some of her writing for this narrative.

Margo Schwadron, a National Park Service archaeologist since 1991, specializes in studying the
relationship between environment and community, with particular focus on the prehistoric set-
tlements in the Ten Thousand Islands. Her investigations have included unique shell ring sites,
large shell islands, and the Turner River mounds. She has submitted a successful application to
have the sites named collectively "The Ten Thousand Islands Archaeological District" and listed on
the National Register of Historic Places. We interviewed Margo on the dock at Gulf Coast Visitor
Center, during the course of boat travel and a trek on the Turner River Mounds, and at the Havana
Cafe in Chokoloskee.

Rick and Jean Seavey, in their role as volunteer researchers in Everglades National Park, have made themselves expert lichenologists, as they have worked to develop the first comprehensive survey of lichens in the park and a corresponding database for future researchers. In addition to lab work and fieldwork for the survey, they do extensive hiking into remote backcountry areas, including the mangroves. In their laboratory in the park located on Research Road, they spoke of their work and also their joy in wilderness.

Skip Snow, retired from a career in the National Park Service, has engaged with backcountry spaces and with the Everglades' wildlife in a number of capacities. He has achieved public renown for his work with pythons in the Everglades. He continues to work on special projects in the park. Skip was interviewed at the Pine Island Chickee.

Tony Terry "fell in love with" South Florida as a young man and decided to stay. Recently retired, he spent his entire law enforcement career in and around the mangrove areas of Flamingo in Everglades National Park. Often, when not on duty, he headed back into the mangroves to fish. An animated storyteller, Tony recounted adventures and contemplations during an interview at his office in Flamingo.

Wanda Brown Townsend was born in 1933 on Chokoloskee Island. She lived on the island for fifty-seven years, marrying James Townsend in 1953 and raising two children, Kelvin and Belinda. Wanda is a lifelong member of the Church of God and is thankful that she grew up on Chokoloskee in the "good old days" before the road, electricity, and telephone changed life on the island forever.

William G. Truesdell became a ranger in Everglades National Park in 1967. Within a few years of his arrival, the ninety-nine-mile Everglades Wilderness Waterway trail from Everglades City through Gulf Coast mangroves to Flamingo was completed and opened to the public. His 1968 spiral-bound guidebook, including strip maps and photos, remained the only guide specifically dedicated to the Waterway until 2011. Since Truesdell's retirement from his position as chief of interpretation at Joshua Tree National Park, he has remained an active naturalist and volunteer. He was interviewed, along with his wife, Kathy, at his home in Twentynine Palms, California.

THE AUTHORS

Anne McCrary Sullivan grew up on the coast of North Carolina and has lived in Florida for more than thirty years. A Florida Master Naturalist with an MFA in poetry, she has been artist in residence in Everglades National Park, Big Cypress National Preserve, and at the Hambidge Center in Georgia. She has articles, chapters, and poems in many literary and academic publications and is author of *Ecology II: Throat Song from the Everglades* (poems) and coauthor of *Paddling the Everglades Wilderness Waterway*. She holds a PhD in English education from the University of Florida, has been poetry editor of *the English Journal* and a Fulbright Scholar in Nigeria. She lives on the Gulf Coast of Florida and spends as much time as possible in the Everglades.

Holly Genzen is a Florida Master Naturalist and an outdoor education specialist. She has a masters in outdoor education and a PhD in educational administration. She has completed a solo thru-hike of the Appalachian Trail and has paddled more than a thousand miles in Central and South Florida. She is coauthor of the guidebook, *Paddling the Everglades Wilderness Waterway*, an effort that required extensive research into the social and natural history of the area. Her experiences in natural Florida have been the inspiration for her artwork, both in paintings and in her daily nature sketchbook. She has also been a volunteer at Shenandoah National Park. Central Florida is currently her home base for adventures in all directions.

ACKNOWLEDGMENTS

Our deepest appreciation goes to our storytellers who shared experiences with generous enthusiasm, sometimes in multiple sessions, one person often leading us to another: "You should talk to . . ." We treasure the hours spent with them in parks and at campsites, kitchen tables, front porches, picnic tables, and workplaces.

We are grateful for the guidance and support of employees and volunteers of Everglades National Park and Big Cypress, especially Bob Showler in the Flamingo District and Alan Scott in the Pine Island District. At Gulf Coast, we are indebted to Joe Sterchele and Margaret Barse in the visitor center, and to boat pilots Mark and David, who took us to the Turner River Mounds. Our appreciation also goes to Bonnie Ciolino and Nancy Russell for their assistance with Chief Naturalist Reports at the Everglades National Park Archives.

Carolyn Thompson and Kenny Brown, lifelong residents of Everglades City, have offered us good company and conversation. They have deep stories, which we hope to find in their own books soon. Carolyn, get those journals out from under the bed! Kenny, keep that manuscript going.

We are indebted to Peter Machonis for his valuable comments on an early draft as well as suggestions from an anonymous reviewer. Al Krizan's enthusiasm for the project and his excellent advice marked a turning point for which we are very grateful. We have been lucky to have the enthusiastic guidance of a fabulous team at Globe Pequot/Pineapple Press: Debra Murphy and Amy Lyons, our editors, and Elaine McGarraugh and Alyssa Messenger.

We owe a special thank you to Pauline Horton for messages, photocopies, handmade soap and, most especially, lemon cookies; to Jolyon Sullivan for lending his array of Nikon lenses to the project and for his generosity of spirit when one of those lenses was drowned at Crooked Creek; and to our families and friends, whose enthusiasm and moral support have accompanied us through the long process of writing this book.

Throughout this process, we have been mindful of those who came to these mangroves before us, those whose voices have gone silent and whose stories will never be told—the early Glades People and the Calusa, who formed the shell mounds and shaped the channels around them, who knew this water/landscape, more intimately than any of us possibly can. We are grateful.

INDEX OF PLACE NAMES

Turtle tracks in the sand at Picnic Key. Photograph by Holly Genzen.